The Metalworker's Workshop

Harold Hall

Special Interest Model Books

Special Interest Model Books Ltd
P.O. Box 327
Poole, Dorset BH15 2RG
England

First published 2010
Text © 2010 Harold Hall
Layout © 2010
Special Interest Model Books Ltd

ISBN 978 185486 256 3

www.specialinterestmodelbooks.co.uk

Printed and bound in the UK by
MPG Books Ltd

Contents

Chapter 1 The purpose of the workshop – 9

The possibilities: Model engineering and workshop equipment; Restoration; Clock-making; Pot-luck Questions to ask yourself; Major machines; Lathe and drilling machine; Band saw; Milling machine; Minor machines; Fittings.

Chapter 2 The workshop – 15

A room in the house; The garage; A purpose-built workshop; Location; Windows; Insulation; Condensation – Temperature difference; Surface condition; Moisture content of the air; Roofing.

Chapter 3 Fittings – 21

Furniture; Benches; Storage; Electricity supply to the workshop; Some pointers; Supply source; Cabling – Length of cable; Electricity in the workshop; Workshop consumer unit; Circuits; Diversity; Earthing; Residual current device; Installation; Lighting; Heating.

Chapter 4 Planning – 33

Metric or imperial? Drill sizes; Thread systems; Calibrated equipment; Metric measuring equipment; Material specifications; Steel – General-purpose steel; Lead content; Non-ferrous metals; Project planning; Study the drawings; Tolerances; Listing your materials; Saving time – Working in parallel; Tool changes; Drawings; Computer-aided design (CAD); Completing the project.

Chapter 5 Hand tools – 41

Files Scrapers; Spanners; Hexagon wrenches; Measuring and marking-out equipment; Centre punches; Callipers and dividers; Depth gauge/ Protractor; Combination square set; Marking out; Hand stamps.

Chapter 6 Precision tools – 51

Micrometers; Vernier callipers; Height gauges; Dial-type measuring instruments; Dial gauges; Dial test indicators; Digital versions; Slip gauges; Sine bars; Hole gauges; Precision spirit level; Parallels; Fixed width parallels; Block parallels; "Wavy" parallels; Adjustable parallels; Surface plates; V blocks.

Chapter 7 Shop-made tools – 63

Saddle stop; Tapping guides; Universal joints; Distance gauges; Grinding rest; Back stop; Faceplate-balancing fixture.

Chapter 8 Electrics and electronics – 69

Machine controls; No volt release; Foot switch; In the workshop; Variable speed drives; Digital read-outs; CAD/CAM/CNC; CAD for drawing only; Reliability.

Chapter 9 Machine installation and safety equipment – 75

Machine installation; Lathe installation; Safety equipment; Face protection; Machine guards; Safety shoes; Ear defenders.

Chapter 10 The lathe – 79

Lathe-only user; The lathe (with milling machine); Size; Speed range; Drive clutch; Top slide; Screw cutting; Saddle half nut; Thread dial indicator; Powered cross slide feed; Milling head.

Chapter 11 Lathe accessories – 87

Cutters; Replaceable tip cutters; Permanently tipped cutters; High-speed steel (HSS) cutters; Which to choose? Tool holders; Work holders; Faceplates; Jawed chucks; The jaws; Backplates; Collet chucks; Gripping range; Closing method; Dead length systems; Collet holders; Worthwhile? "Must haves"; Drill chucks; Centres; Catch plate and lathe dog; Tailstock die holders; Steadies; Fixed steadies; Travelling steadies; Knurling tools; Saddle stop; Other accessories; Tailstock; Back stop; Coolant pump; Keats angle plate; Non-turning operations; Boring; Dividing.

Chapter 12 The drilling machine and accessories – 105

The machine; Mounting; Speed range; Other features; Controls; Accessories; Drills; Jobber drills; Blacksmith drills; Stub drills; Countersinks; Counterbores; Vice; Compound table; Other accessories; Using a drilling machine.

Chapter 13 The milling machine – 115

Turret mills; Mill/Drills; Common features; Speed control; Speed ranges; Rotating head; Calibrated X, Y and Z feeds; Digital read-outs; Traverse stops; Power feed; Draw bar; Spindle taper; Horizontal/Vertical attachments.

Chapter 14 Milling machine accessories – 121

Cutters with shanks; The non–working end; The working end; Indexable cutters; Solid cutters; Which size? Plain or threaded? Other types; Disk-type cutters; Cutter holders; Boring head; Minor accessories; Machine vice – Considerations; Angle plates; Parallels; V blocks; Positioning devices Major accessories; Dividing heads; 5C fixtures; Rotary tables; Taking a cut is easy.

Chapter 15 Grinders and motorised saws – 139

Grinders; Off-hand grinders; Tool and cutter grinder; Surface grinder; Belt and disk sanders; Motorised saws; Hack saw; Horizontal band saw; Fret saw.

Chapter 16 Presses, sheet metal machines, welders and shapers – 147

Presses; Uses; Bending; Punching holes; Cropping; Force fitting and removing; Types; Fly presses; Arbor presses; Hydraulic presses; Accessories; Punches and dies; Bending; Installation; Need for? Sheet metal machines; Welders: Electric welding equipment; Arc welders; Metal inert gas welders; Safety equipment Shapers.

Final comments – 159
Information – 159

Author's preface

I have written this book primarily, but by no means exclusively, for the benefit of readers in the early stages of setting up a metalworking workshop, including those who have had a lathe for many years but now find it possible to expand their workshop facilities.

During my time as editor of the *Model Engineers' Workshop (MEW)* magazine, and from subsequent observations, I have been surprised to find how many model engineers have no access to a workshop, either at home or even via a college-based course. If you add to this the number of people who have just a lathe and a few hand tools, and are based in the corner of the garage or the garden shed, then the total is not inconsiderable. Whilst I consider that these people will have the most to gain from reading this book, it will also have much of interest to those fortunate readers who consider their workshop to be well, but not fully, equipped.

Do not be misled by the title. This book is not just about building a workshop, but includes everything that goes to make a well-equipped set-up.

Harold Hall, 2009

Chapter 1

The purpose of the workshop

Once you have decided that setting up a metalworking workshop will provide you with the facilities for an interesting pastime, you will naturally be keen to make progress with the idea quickly. However, there is no point in purchasing a lathe if you do not have a suitable place to house it and so, even before establishing a workshop, you need to decide what your workshop's ultimate activity will be. From this, you can establish what equipment you will need, which will largely determine the workshop's size, although I do appreciate that some readers will already be partway down this road.

The possibilities

The first step is to decide what your workshop will be used for. This may seem an easy question, but many people have set out with the idea of becoming involved in model engineering but have never, or not until very much later, come anywhere near achieving this aim. (I, for one, have almost fallen into the "never" category"!) So first endeavour to pinpoint your idea for the workshop's purpose and then ask yourself whether the idea is really viable. What are the possibilities?

Model engineering and workshop equipment

Model engineering obviously comes to mind, but reader surveys have shown that this is not the predominant workshop activity undertaken by most workshop owners, albeit by a substantial number. Making workshop equipment is obviously a major interest and is probably the easiest to take up because many projects need only a limited number of man-hours to complete. It can also be made on equipment that fits the stereotype of the size of machines required in a workshop.

Restoration

Restoration is a wide-ranging activity, with motorcycles and cars predominating (**Photo 1**), although I also know of people involved with full-size locomotives, stationary steam engines, etc. If cars or motorcycles are your intended interest, then your choice of workshop and tools will differ markedly from those used for other interests, with welding and spray-painting being typically more prominent.

Restoration is not confined to larger items, and clockwork toys, etc. are also of interest. Many

1. A 1935 Morris 8, Series 1, being restored in the workshop of Frank Darby.

of these items are in a sorry state of repair due to the nature of their former owners. However, they present a wide range of metalworking activities, such as turning, milling, gear-cutting, tinplate-forming and painting. Also, if the subject is, say, a locomotive, it will need to be painted and lined in a colour that matches the full-size item. As the paint will no longer be commercially available, it may have to be specially mixed in the workshop, which all adds up to an interesting but demanding hobby. One advantage of working at scales such as these is that the machines and workshop need only be small.

Clock restoration is a similar activity, without the painting, but including some woodwork in repairing cabinets.

Before finally deciding to become involved in a particular restoration subject, do establish contact with others who share a similar interest and/or with any national association. This is particularly important if you have a very specific interest. A senior member of the Brough Superior motorcycle club stated, during a visit, that restoration had almost ceased because the chances of finding a specimen to restore had become increasingly unlikely.

Clock-making

Clock-making is another possibility, and the main items of equipment are not that different from those for model engineering or tool-making. However, it is best to purchase the lathe and other items with this purpose in mind because there are some unique requirements.

Pot luck

Of course, you may prefer just to set up a metalworking workshop and see what turns up to be worked on. I have known some people who have repaired a local church clock, which may not have worked for decades. What could be more rewarding? Others have made parts for local firms and other home workshop owners, some turning this into a small business. The list is a long one, so give it a lot of thought.

Questions to ask yourself

Once you have made your initial choice, the next question is: how much time do you have available to regularly spend on a project? If you can spare only two or three hours a week on average, do you have sufficient patience to work on the same project over many years? This is what you will have to do if your project is a locomotive, even if in the smaller scales, or a large-scale restoration of a vintage car.

If your answer to both the above is "yes", then in what scale do you expect to work? If, for example, you choose to work on the larger sizes of locomotive or traction engine, then the average 3 1/2in. centre lathe will not be ideal and a larger size will be preferable, as will a large-size milling machine. Likewise, a vintage car will need housing both during its repair and after completion. In this case, will you be able to provide a workshop large enough to house such equipment and the items you are working on? If "yes" again, you must answer the final question: will you have the cash to finance the project?

I suspect that many people will answer "no" to at least one of the questions, and they will have to consider lesser projects. For some, these will be items of workshop equipment that will take from only a few hours to a few tens of hours. In this case, you will quite rapidly have the satisfaction of seeing a completed project and the even more satisfying pleasure of putting it to use on subsequent projects. Similarly, if model engineering appeals, then a small stationary steam engine, like the example in **Photo 2**, can be completed and on display in a few tens of hours.

The restoration of an antique clock or a clockwork toy can also be completed in much less than a year at only a few hours a week. Do not put off making a start just because it is not possible to make that 1/4-scale traction engine, as you had so dearly wished to do. Many people have had to delay such ambitions, sometimes until retirement, but have gained much satisfaction from making smaller items on the way, as well as experience for the more advanced projects that they eventually undertake.

Major machines
Once you have decided on your intended interest, you should make a list of the major machines that you require, although it is not necessary to specify make and model at this stage. This is not straightforward because

2. A small stationary steam engine is a good subject if you are a beginner or have limited time.

you do not want to end up with an expensive machine that hardly gets used, or get well into a project and wish you had space for some other or larger item. Space to me is crucial, even more so than finance; finance may eventually become available but increasing the size of a workshop to house another machine may be a daunting prospect, if not all but impossible.

I cannot be exact about the machines required because there are many varying factors, depending on the activity chosen. For example, if clock-making is your chosen direction, then welding will be low on your list of priorities, but for restoration of cars or motorcycles it would be quite high.

Each of the following machines is discussed in much greater detail in later chapters.

Lathe and drilling machine
A lathe, I feel, should be number one on the list in most cases and many workshop owners produce interesting work with no other machine. Within size limits, milling is quite possible, as illustrated in **Photo 3**. Also, with a drill chuck in the lathe's spindle and the

faceplate mounted on the tailstock, you have a form of horizontal drilling machine. In this case the workpiece is being fed rather than the drill (**Photo 4**). However, as drilling machines are relatively small and cheap, using the lathe for drilling should be a last resort. Because of this, I consider a drilling machine to be almost essential, although I know of someone who has worked without one for many years.

Band saw

You might expect a milling machine to come next, but this is not the case. Although not as essential as the lathe and the drilling machine, I would next add a horizontal/universal band saw (**Photo 5**). The economy versions of these, now widely available, first appeared on the market just before I became editor of *MEW*. When visiting reader's workshops, I was

3. If your chosen activity is confined to the smaller scales, a milling machine is far from essential, as this photo of milling being undertaken on the lathe shows.

4. Drilling can be carried out on the lathe, although a small drilling machine is preferable.

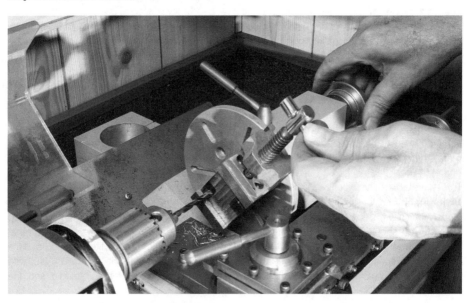

5. A universal band saw will avoid the need for much manual sawing (Chester).

6. A typical mill/drill (Warco).

surprised by just how many people had already acquired one and how many commented on their considerable benefit to the workshop's activities.

Without some form of powered saw, the prospect of manually cutting off a few billets, say from a 50mm diameter bar of steel, would be a considerable deterrent from starting a project. My minimum workshop would therefore definitely include a lathe, drilling machine and a band saw (or powered hack saw or similar, see Chapter 15).

Milling machine

Finally, in terms of major machines (although others, such as a shaper and a surface grinder, may appear on some workshop-owners' lists), there is the milling machine. For almost all tasks a vertical mill is to be preferred, whether this is one of the popular mill/drills (**Photo 6**) or a genuine vertical mill (**Photo 7**), probably an industrial-calibre machine. Horizontal milling machines have limited applications and most workshops will function perfectly well without one.

In general, the facilities required on the above machines will be the same no matter what type of project they are intended for; only the size will differ. However, if you intend to take up clock-making, which involves working at smaller diameters, you will need a lathe that runs at higher speeds than those usually provided. Also, because of the need for concentricity for the many small spindles involved, it is usual to have a lathe equipped with a range of collet chucks would be the norm.

Each of these workshop machines is discussed in greater detail in later chapters.

8. An off-hand grinder, although not ideal, is likely to be the only facility for sharpening workshop tools. However, making a few simple accessories will largely overcome its limitations (Warco).

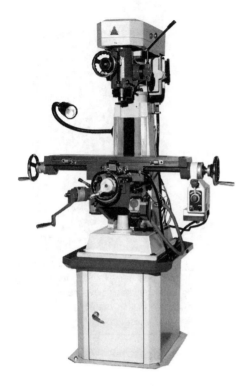

7. A typical turret mill (Chester UK Ltd).

Minor machines

The only other 'must have' machine is an off-hand grinder (**Photo 8**) for grinding and sharpening tasks, although its performance with regard to sharpening is very limited.

Fittings

The contents of the workshop do not stop at the machines, and bench space will obviously have to be provided. For most normal activities, I would suggest at least a 2 m length of clear bench top, preferably in one span, for day-to-day working. Of course, this again depends on the intended use; for example, if the intended project is relatively large, you may need an additional bench solely to store the item while work is in progress.

Storage space is another requirement, but this can be mostly beneath the benches and even beneath the machine tools if they are bench-mounted. If your restoration project is a motorcycle or car, and this is to be stored in the workshop, then a large area of floor space will be essential.

Again, the above comments are brief at this stage, as most issues will be dealt with in much more detail throughout the book.

Chapter 2

The workshop

Once you have decided on the workshop's major items, you can establish its size, although I suspect you may eventually wish you had made it a little larger. You can then consider your options.

Probably the best method of establishing the size is to make paper cut-outs of each major item. These need not be too detailed – basic rectangles will suffice – but be sure to allow for access at the sides, for example, for opening the lathe's changewheel cover and for the movement of the milling machine's table. You can then move these cut-outs around until you find the best layout, from which you can determine the workshop size. If you have access to a computer with a computer-aided design (CAD) program, you can use the same

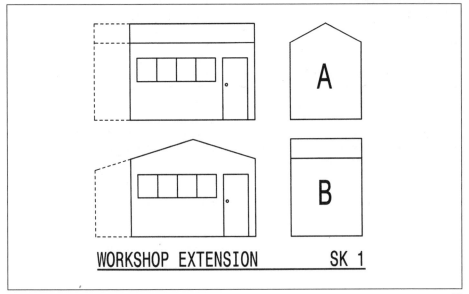

WORKSHOP EXTENSION   SK 1

approach, with the added advantage of being able to print out the result.

However, I am fully aware that other factors, not directly related to the workshop's contents, may have a major bearing on your decision, such as available space, finance and time. You may even have to backtrack and ask yourself what you wish to use the workshop for.

Unfortunately, apart from making temporary use of a garage or garden shed for a few years, setting up a workshop is a decision that can be difficult to change later. Buying a bigger shed may be no more expensive than buying a bigger lathe, but it involves considerably more work. It therefore pays to think very carefully about the form the workshop will take and to consider the possibility of a future extension. Sk. 1 shows how workshop A would be more practical to extend than workshop B.

Apart from any temporary location, you probably have three options:

1. a room in the house
2. the garage
3. a purpose-built wooden or brick building.

A room in the house
A room in the house is an option for only a few people, although the smaller the set-up the more likely that it will be practical. However, I have seen very satisfactory workshop set-ups like this. You would need to consider the volume of noise generated and, if an upstairs room, the strength of the floor.

The garage
In my opinion, the garage, although an option adopted by many people, is only completely acceptable if the car is left outside. The presence of a car, often brought in damp, is a recipe for disaster. Also, providing background heating to avoid condensation and rust, and increased heating while working, is expensive, and the loss of heat through an ill-fitting garage door and its single-steel construction is a particular problem.

If you decide to use the garage, without car, then the size will be fixed, although this is unlikely to be a problem because even the smallest garage is more than large enough for all but the largest machines. The main door should be boarded over to prevent draughts and to insulate against heat loss. If this is the only entrance, you can overcome the problem by installing a screen with a single door, thus dividing the garage into two. The outer section can then be used for storage while the inner section can be used for the machines, etc. – and being smaller than the whole garage will be easier to heat. Boarding under the roof joists will improve insulation and appearance and, if painted white, will improve the lighting (natural light may be limited or non-existent).

To minimise the problem of rust, the floor and walls should be painted with a waterproof paint to act as a vapour barrier, and background heating should be installed to maintain a minimum temperature of 8°C. Once these provisions have been met, and with a solid floor, robust walls and good headroom, your workshop will be the envy of many.

Shame about the car though! Despite my reservations, I am fully aware that many people do good work in a garage shared with a car. I carry out my cabinet-making activities in such a set-up, but the car is left outside the garage while I am doing so. I also attempt to avoid working there in the depth of winter.

A purpose-built workshop
A purpose-built workshop may be a wooden shed or a pre-cast concrete or brick building,

although in some conservation areas there will be constraints on what is permitted. Even for a wooden shed I would strongly advise using a concrete base for the floor, and even a wooden floor should still rest on a concrete base, suitably protected from rising damp.

If you have decided on a purpose-built workshop, I am sure you have already thought about its location, but you will now need to make a final decision. You can then turn your attention to other considerations.

Location
If you are fortunate enough to have a large garden, a workshop at the furthest point from the house may be less intrusive but it can involve a long run for the power cable. Placing the cable underground, as stipulated in the regulations, is really the only acceptable method. However, if the workshop is adjacent to the house, then an overhead cable with catenary support is an option.

Windows
The position of the windows is also worth considering, although not only for the most obvious reason, which, ideally, is to provide sufficient daylight for most of the work to be carried out without artificial lighting. However, their position can also have a marked effect on whether condensation occurs on your machine tools.

When I was working away from home during the day, I was puzzled to find that condensation sometimes caused rust to form on my machines and stock materials, etc., but at other times all would be OK for a while, until the same thing happened again without warning. However, once I started to work at home the reason became obvious when, on entering my workshop one morning, I was surprised to find much of it covered in a fine film of condensation.

The large windows in my workshop faced the mid-morning sun, which had suddenly broken through after a period of cloud. As a result of the previous very cold night, my tooling was quite cold, despite the background heating. The rapid rise in air temperature due to the sudden appearance of the sun could not be matched by the surface temperature of the machines and, as a result of the increased temperature difference, condensation occurred (see below). The lesson, therefore, is not to position your windows facing the sun if it can be avoided. My solution was to fit blinds and increase the background heating a little, an arrangement that has reduced the problem appreciably.

Bright sunlight also affects your vision as you move between brightly lit and shaded areas of the workshop.

Insulation
You can reduce heat loss by lining both the walls and the ceiling with a layer of insulation. Expanded polystyrene sheeting is the easiest form of insulation to use. This can be cut to size with a sharp knife and, if cut a little on the large side, can be pressed into the spaces in the workshop's frame, where it will hold itself in place while the lining board is fixed into position.

There is a large range of lining materials for walls but I would suggest MDF (medium-density fibreboard). Ideally, paint this with a gloss paint to provide a vapour barrier. Alternatively, use board that already has some sort of waterproof coating on one face and position it with this face open to the workshop.

Condensation
The following is a brief explanation of a subject that is much more complex than most people perceive. Three factors have a bearing on the development of condensation:

1. temperature difference, i.e. the difference between the temperature of the air and that of the item on which condensation may occur
2. surface condition
3. moisture content of the air, i.e. the humidity

Temperature difference
This factor is the easiest to control but can be expensive as it requires the workshop to be maintained at a sufficiently high temperature to avoid large temperature swings and, thereby, large temperature differences.

Surface condition
Surface condition is also easy to control but needs constant attention. There will be variations in the surfaces of purchased items, for example, a polished surface or a matt finish, but the application of an oil film is the responsibility of the workshop owner. An oil film has two effects:

1. it reduces the likelihood of condensation
2. if condensation does occur, it acts as a barrier between the steel and the moisture.

Unfortunately, working with heavily oiled machines and tools is not pleasant, and they often require cleaning before being used. The oil film also needs to be re-applied after use, which requires a discipline that many of us would admit to overlooking.

An alternative to an oil coating, but one that is only suitable for use on flat surfaces, is the lubricating wax used by cabinet-makers on their machine tables to enable the easier movement of timber across the surface. As well as acting as a lubricant, this wax also inhibits condensation. For example, my band saw and planer-thicknesser tables, which are both cast iron and share the garage with my car, are still free of rust after about six years, even without any background heating.

A very thin film of oil, applied with a lightly oiled cloth, will help appreciably if used with background heating, and the tools will still be acceptable to work with in this condition. Newly finished parts, if machined dry, are particularly prone to rust and will benefit if treated in this way.

Moisture content of the air
Humidity, i.e. the moisture content of the air, is much more of a problem, and the only way of directly controlling it is to use a dehumidifier. However, there are steps that can be taken to minimise the problem (see below).

First, we will return to the question of temperature difference. Starting from, say, mid-afternoon, when there will probably have been a period of near-constant air temperature, during which the machines' surface temperature will have stabilised to approximately the same as that of the air, the following sequence occurs.

As the day progresses, the air temperature starts to fall but the temperature of the mass of the metal, which takes some time to respond, will lag behind that of the air. The surfaces therefore remain marginally warmer than the air until the temperature stabilises at its lowest value, i.e. that set by the background heating. During this time, the surface is warmer than the air, so condensation cannot occur, which is why it does not occur during the night.

The next morning, the air temperature in the workshop will begin to rise in response to the external ambient temperature; at this point, the machines' surface temperature will again lag behind, but this time it will be colder than the air temperature. As long as the rate of rise is slow, the temperature difference will be small and condensation will not occur. However, the precise difference between air and surface temperatures at which condensation occurs (known as the "dew point") also depends on the moisture content of the air: the more moisture in the air, the lower the temperature difference required for condensation to develop. Moreover, the warmer the air, the greater the amount of moisture that it can carry. Who has heard of a cold muggy day?

From the above, we can see that the critical point occurs when there is a relatively rapid rise in workshop temperature. This can be caused by:

1. the workshop owner switching on additional heating in preparation for a period of workshop activity
2. a rise in temperature due to external conditions (as mentioned above).

Also from the above, we can see that, as the temperature rises, the air will attempt to take up more moisture – but from where you may ask. The answer is: mostly from the fabric of the building and its fittings. This is why it is so desirable that the internal surface of the workshop has a vapour barrier, such as a coat of gloss paint, or is lined with waterproofed boarding (see above). This also applies to the materials used in other items, such as concrete or wooden flooring, wooden or metal shelving and benches – even the cloth in workshop overalls or dust sheets.

Assuming there is no moisture entry through the walls, etc., it is also worth bearing in mind that the internal fabric of the building gains most of its moisture content during the humid summer months. This means that late autumn/early winter is the most likely time for condensation to occur, as anyone who has an indoor hygrometer will be aware. Consequently, it may be advisable to turn up the background heating by a few degrees during this time.

Roofing

Finally, remember that your workshop, with all its valuable tooling, is a long-term investment, and use the best and most long-lasting roofing material available. Traditional roofing felt, which was once the only option and needed frequent renewal, is no longer recommended.

Chapter 3

Fittings

Once you have established the shell of the workshop, the next stage is to equip it with the necessary fitments in preparation for adding your chosen tools and machinery.

These include such items as benches, shelves, electrical power sockets and lighting.

Furniture

Benches

Once you have chosen the machines, you will need to decide whether to purchase them with their own stand or to place them on the

1. Benches made of melamine-faced chipboard. Note the piece of flat-bottomed guttering (right), which is being used to provide pull-out "drawers" for material storage.

workshop's benches. If you have chosen machines at the smaller end of the range, then the latter is to be preferred because, with a longer bench, it is easier to divide the space beneath to provide storage room. It also gives you greater flexibility, so that you can change the position of the machines if necessary. However, larger lathes have special installation requirements (see Chapter 9) and particularly strong bench tops are required. Because of this, the manufacturer's stands are to be preferred.

Once you have decided on the size and position of the bench, or benches, your next consideration is their method of construction. The traditional table-type bench, with four or more legs and built-in shelves, may once have been the norm, but there is a lot to be said for a more modern approach. In Chapter 2, it was explained how the materials used in the construction of the workshop take up and retain moisture from the air in the workshop but then releasing it when the temperature rises, thus increasing the likelihood of condensation. This situation can be minimised by constructing them from materials such as melamine-faced chipboard (Photo 1).

This type of bench can be made very simply by using the plastic joiner blocks commonly available from DIY stores, but do use a sufficient number to support the heavy weights that are likely. An alternative to joiner blocks, and probably preferable, is to use timber strips of, say, 20mm × 20mm cross-section. The dividers between each section of the bench will provide rigidity from back to front, but the purely open construction will allow the bench to swing from side to side. To prevent this, the bench should either have a back made from similar board or be anchored to the structure of the workshop. If you are intending to fit a bench vice, anchoring will certainly be preferable because of the nature of some tasks you are

likely to undertake with the vice, typically the bending of steel bars. A fly press, or similar, will also exert forces on the bench that will make a rigidly fixed bench a must!

In the bench shown in Photo 1, the shelves have been omitted from one section in order to provide knee space for sitting at the bench when carrying out light-duty tasks, such as drawing, assembly, painting, etc. It also provides storage space for the workshop vacuum cleaner!

An idea for the bench top that I have adopted from one of the workshops I have visited is to use flooring-grade chipboard, which can be obtained in a light green colour (I am not sure about the significance of this). Coating this with, say, three coats of polyurethane varnish will give it a hard-wearing and pleasing dark green surface. When this becomes worn, it can be sanded and varnished again, bringing it back to its original state. For added strength, battens should be added below the bench top, say four of 69mm × 34mm cross-section. An alternative is to use a kitchen worktop from a DIY outlet; these are often damaged in storage and can often be purchased at a favourable price.

You may like to consider adding doors to the bench (**Photo 2**). However, although doors would be considered essential in a woodworking workshop, to keep out the dust that is produced, they are of limited importance in the metalworking workshop. Even so, the presence of doors gives a tidy appearance and, of more practical importance, the inside surfaces of the doors can be used for additional storage (**Photo 3**).

Storage

Shelves below the benches will probably provide the bulk of the storage space but, being deep and with low-level access, this

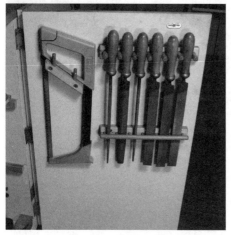

4. Shallow eye-level shelves are useful for storing small or frequently used items.

2./3. Doors on benches present a tidy appearance and can provide additional storage facilities

can be somewhat restricted. With this in mind, shallower shelves above the bench will be very useful, and will make smaller and more frequently used items more readily available (**Photo 4**).

If, like me on one occasion, you are building your own timber workshop, you might like to consider the following for one wall. Rather than using a frame of, say, 44mm × 34mm, make the uprights from 144mm × 18mm, spaced at 600mm intervals. You can then drill these

uprights at intervals and insert pegs on which to place the shelves (**Photo 5**). As the pegs are removable, you can modify the spacing of the shelves to suit the items placed on them; this system works very well.

Plastic bins are also very useful for storage, but their louvred mounting panels can be costly and, more importantly, too large for the available space. An alternative, which I have used successfully, is a row of large-headed roofing-felt nails, not driven fully home. A series of small holes, drilled at intervals in a piece of melamine-faced chipboard, will ensure that the nails are in line and enter squarely. Using three nails to the small bin has worked without a problem for me and is a perfectly adequate alternative.

The storage of materials is a major problem because you will be dealing with pieces of all lengths. Making a honeycomb of closely packed shelves may seem like a good idea, but shorter lengths will inevitably be pushed to the back of the shelf, so they cannot be retrieved without removing all the pieces. However, this problem is easily resolved. Purchase a length or two of flat-bottomed guttering and cut them

5. The main frame of one end of this wooden workshop is made from 144mm × 18mm timber, proving an ideal means of supporting shelves.

to lengths in which to store your material. These can be pulled out like drawers in order to retrieve lengths that have worked their way to the back. An example of this was shown in Photo 1.

Smaller machines may suggest that a smaller workshop will suffice. Whilst this is undoubtedly true up to a point, the space required by the peripheral items will not diminish to the same extent. Typically, the bench vice will need just as much room, and no doubt, there will be just as many drills, taps, nuts, screws and washers, etc. to store away. If the workshop size has to be kept to a minimum, then it becomes increasingly important to make full use of the space available. There are three possible approaches to this problem:

1. Store items on the rear of the doors, as already shown in Photo 3.

2. Replace the plinth board with drawers, as shown in Photo 6. Fitting small wheels to the rear corners of these drawers, so that they run on the workshop floor, will make them easier to open and close.

3. Make pull-out trays between the bench-top battens for storing smaller-size materials (**Photo 7**). In this particular workshop, the trays are about 1.5m long and the workshop door has to be opened to allow them to be withdrawn fully.

You will doubtless find it desirable to have some useful data readily available in the workshop, and this will necessitate storing a few books. However, there are some items of data, such as tapping drill sizes, which you will need to refer to frequently. For these, provide yourself with a notice board on which you can pin photocopies of your most frequently used data. The rear of the workshop door, which cannot be

6. Drawers in place of plinth boards provide additional storage.

7. A method of storing smaller material sizes.

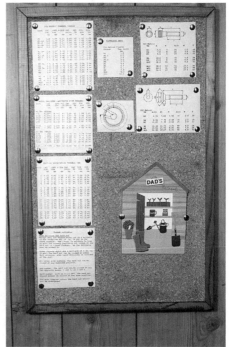

8. A notice board is useful for displaying frequently required data, e.g. tapping drill sizes, and if mounted on the workshop door, does not take up space that would be more useful for other things.

Electricity supply to the workshop

We now come to the complex subject of electrical installations. First, I must stress, do not attempt to bypass the system. Few people would argue against using a registered fitter for gas installation and, whilst a gas explosion is immediately spectacular, an electrical fire can be equally devastating.

I am not suggesting that an electrical installation cannot be done by the workshop owner because the practical side of doing this is certainly much easier than with gas. However, the technical side is far more complex and

easily used for anything else, is a good place to position this (**Photo 8**). In fact, it is the only space available in my workshop as all the walls are covered with shelving. In this respect, the more storage space you have the easier it is to keep the workshop tidy.

open to error, so do seek advice regarding the latest regulations, even if you eventually do the work yourself.

A visit to the local library is a good starting point and, whilst the main regulations can be lengthy and complex, simplified versions that apply to the more common applications are frequently produced. The Internet is also a mine of information, and there are numerous books on the subject.

Some pointers

As readers will realize, in this book it is quite impossible to cover in full the requirements laid down by the various regulations, not least because it will be read internationally. However, the following are some pointers that should help you to understand the basic requirements before attempting to delve deeper into the regulations, either from published material, or in consultation with an electrical installation engineer.

Supply source

Preferably, a separate switch fuse or circuit breaker should be installed at your main property's incoming supply for supplying the workshop. However, as there will be no switch between this and the mains, it will be necessary to get the supply company to remove their incoming fuses in order to allow this connection to be made safely. An alternative, although not recommended unless your workshop and machines are very small, is to use a spare way in the property's consumer unit. Do not feed your workshop from one of the property's household sockets because this will severely limit the amount of current available!

Cabling

Once you have established your supply, the next step is to install the cabling in order get it into the workshop. Three things need careful consideration:

1. where the cable will run
2. the type of cable to use
3 the cross-section of the cable.

In simple terms, the cable can run either above ground or below ground. If above ground, the cable will have to be at a minimum height and, unless it is very short, it must be supported with a catenary support cable. If below ground, the cable will have to be at a minimum depth, with, I believe some warning tape installed just above it.

Unless there is some additional protection, it is essential to use a wire-armoured cable below ground and, in any case, it is much easier to install. This type of cable has a single layer of armour, with a plastic outer sheath; I believe double-armoured cable is available for particularly adverse conditions. Above ground, wire-armoured cable is still the best approach, but if you are using some other type of cable, do check that it will withstand both the summer sun and the winter frosts. Although most cables will do this for a while, they may age prematurely. In the case of single wire-armoured cable below ground, care must be taken to check that the outer sheath is not damaged because this would allow water to gain access to the wire armour, which could then rust; this is particularly important as it is also used as the earth cable.

In the case of an above-ground installation using wire-armoured cable, or protected by some means, such as electrical conduit, the minimum height requirement may not apply. However, it will need to be positioned where mechanical damage is unlikely and sufficiently above soil level to avoid it being accidentally covered if the soil level is raised a little.

The following comments apply to cables in any location, not just the supply cable between the source and the workshop, although the requirements regarding length are unlikely to be of concern for shorter runs.

Do not fall into the trap of thinking that it is solely the core's cross-section that fixes the rating of the cable; this is not the case. As the temperature of the copper conductor will be considerably below its melting point, a sizeable increase in temperature will have no detrimental effect on it. However, increased temperature would be a major problem to the insulation, causing its early failure. Insulation comes in different forms that withstand different temperatures and, as a result, the cable rating will change; therefore do ensure that the data you consult apply to the type of cable you are about to use. The rating tables should also detail the effect of installing the cable in different locations; obviously a cable hidden in the building's insulation will run hotter, requiring it to be limited to a lower maximum current than a cable in the open.

A cable's permitted current-carrying capacity is also dependent on the type of device protecting it: fuse or circuit breaker. Obviously, if the protection device is able to respond more quickly, you can run the cable a little nearer to its limit.

Regarding the wire-armoured cable, you should be aware that the wire armour is also used for the earth return. Because of this, you only need two copper cores in the case of a single-phase supply. I cannot be precise about the number and diameter of the steel strands within an armoured cable, but it will be around 25 strands of about 1mm diameter for the probable size of cable. From this, you can see that it is not possible just to bunch up the strands and add them to a terminal block, as you would for a copper cable. In this case, the cable has to

pass through a special gland that grips the steel strands, thus relieving strain as well as enabling the connection to be made. These are readily available and easy to install.

Length of cable
I think few readers will understand that the amount of current that a cable is permitted to carry also depends on the cable's length. There are two reasons for this.

Probably the easiest to comprehend is that there will be a voltage drop along the length of the cable because of its resistance and the current flowing through it. This will reduce the voltage available at the load end and, in extreme cases, can cause equipment to cease to function properly.

More obscure, but of equal importance, is the effect that the cable's resistance will have on the level of the fault current that will flow under fault conditions. With a short-circuit at the load end, the level of the fault current, normally many times the full load current, will be restricted by the cable's resistance. As the length of the cable increases, the fault current will decrease, increasing the time that the protection device, especially if it is a fuse, will take to interrupt the circuit. In extreme cases, it may not clear the fault, making an electrical fire even more likely.

For these reasons, do ensure that the cable feeding your remote workshop conforms to requirements. Fortunately, unless your workshop is a considerable distance from the source, the size of the cable required is unlikely to increase appreciably; however, if it is close to the limit, it may just move it up to the next size. Do ensure that you check this requirement.

Electricity in the workshop

Workshop consumer unit

With the supply now at the workshop, you will need to distribute it to the various electrical items. Do not rely on the circuit breaker or fuse at the source to protect the workshop as it is there only to protect the supply cable. Treat the workshop as a mini property and install a consumer unit, preferably with circuit breakers rather than fuses, as these give better protection. Circuit breakers also enable individual circuits to be switched off more easily.

Circuits

How you branch the supply from this point will depend on the extent of the workshop's equipment, but I would suggest at least three circuits: one each for lighting, heating and power points. However, whatever number you come up with, do have a minimum of two spare spaces in the unit to allow for future additions. You do not need to include any circuit breakers, only the space for them.

It is essential to keep the lighting circuit separate, because, due to the smaller cables, etc. used within lighting fittings, it needs a lower rated circuit breaker to ensure adequate protection.

Separating the heating and power point circuits is less crucial, but it will make it easier to turn off the background heating during the summer months.

Power points are a complex requirement and you first need to decide how many you require. The cost of a few extra sockets will add little to the overall costs so do err on the generous side. Also, do fit dual sockets in all cases, except perhaps for those feeding the units on the heating circuit. Once you have decided on the number and location, there are two methods of connecting them. The first, which is the most common method in the UK, is the ring connection. With this, the sockets are connected one after the other, with the final one being connected back to source, hence the term "ring". It is also permitted to connect a limited number of sockets, or "spurs", off the ring. You can have more than one ring, fed from separate circuit breakers, if your workshop is large enough for this to be worthwhile.

Note: As I understand, the ring method is rarely used outside the UK because it is dependent on the plugs being fitted with fuses, a feature that is not common elsewhere. Non-UK readers should therefore regard this method with caution.

For a small number of sockets, it may be permissible to connect these only as a spur rather than as a ring, for example, in the heating circuit mentioned above.

The regulations give details of the size of cable to use in these circuits, but they may not be what you would expect. For example, if you have two double 13 amp sockets on a spur, you may think that you need cable with a minimum rating of 52 amps (4 × 13 amps), but this is not the case. On the basis that it is unlikely that all four sockets would be required to provide maximum power at the same time, the regulations permit a lower rated cable; this is called "diversity".

Diversity

It is also necessary to consider whether the level of diversity is appropriate. Consider, for example, a heating circuit (like the above) with three 3kW heaters operated by a single time switch. If this switches on at a time when the workshop is well below the required temperature, then all three will switch on together and remain on for an appreciable time. In this case, the permitted diversity will not apply.

A more extreme case would be if, as a member of the local engineering society, you threw open your workshop to its members for their use. In this case, all your machines could be running at the same time. Whilst I realise this is an unlikely situation, it serves to illustrate a point; in this case, that each machine should be on a separate circuit and fed by its own circuit breaker.

Another example is an electric furnace. This, due to it high current demand, should have its own circuit breaker, in the same way as a domestic oven has its own circuit. If this applies to your situation, you may need to increase the capacity of the supply to your workshop.

Earthing

The provision of an earth connection is far more complex than just driving a spike into the ground – a method commonly used in the past and still used domestically in a very few cases. It is essential that you link into your main property's earthing system, whatever this may be, so do not be tempted to run a two-core cable to the workshop and provide earthing locally via a spike or buried earth plate; this is rarely acceptable.

Note: The term "earth" is misleading because "earth", in the sense of soil, is a very poor conductor, especially if it is dry. So, as far as earthing is concerned, do not rely on the frame of the workshop being in contact with the ground because its inherent resistance will be so high that it may not generate sufficient fault current to trip the protecting device quickly, if at all. Incidentally, any gardeners reading this should ensure that their metal-framed

greenhouse has an equipotential bonding cable if they use electricity to heat and light it.

However, the provision of earthing does not stop at the power points but includes all metalwork that, due to a fault condition, however unlikely, could become connected to the electricity supply.

Let us consider a metal-framed and metal-clad workshop building. Even if this is lined internally with an insulating material, say MDF, the supply cable may have to pass through the outer skin at some point, and an electrical fault between the cable and the building is not out of the question. Therefore, the workshop, and any other major metalwork within it, must be bonded to the earth connections with what are called "equipotential bonding cables".

It may seem that these cables are just there to keep all metalwork parts at nominally zero potential, but this is not the case. Their purpose is to carry the fault current if any part of the metalwork becomes accidentally connected to the main supply. Therefore, they must be able to carry a fault current sufficient to trip the protecting device (fuse or circuit breaker); however, if they are too small, they may disintegrate before the protecting device trips.

Consequently, the equipotential bonding cables must be rated according to the size of the protection device. In the case of a metal-framed building, this will be the size of the fuse or circuit breaker at the source of the supply cable in the main property. However, as the cable will start from zero current and will therefore be cold, and will then only have to carry the current for a short while, it can be smaller than the supply cable; the regulations will give the size required.

The requirements described for a metal-framed building apply equally to any major metal items inside the workshop, such as a metal bench top.

Residual current device

Most readers may consider the purpose of a residual current device (RCD) to be solely to protect the individual from a fatal electric shock but, whilst this is the prime purpose, it is not the only one. First, let us consider in simple terms how RCDs work.

Readers will understand that current flowing down the live wire to the load will then return along the neutral wire back to the supply. The RCD can compare the two currents and, as long as they are equal but flowing in opposite directions, the device will register this as a zero reading. However, if some of the current leaks away to earth at the load, the returning current will be less than the supply current and the RCD will detect the difference and, if it is sufficient, will disconnect the load from the supply.

Let us first consider the aspect of protection from electric shock, because this is where the device needs to be most sensitive. In approximate terms, a current of 2mA flowing through a person's body will be experienced as only a very minor sensation and will in no way be harmful, but this will not be the case with a current of 50mA. From this, it can be seen that the RCD has to be both rapid and sensitive to a very small current difference, very commonly a 30mA operating level.

Unfortunately, electrical insulation is not perfect, either inherently or due to contamination, and a very small leakage of current will be inevitable. This is generally so low that, individually, the 30mA switching level will not be reached by a large margin. However, where the RCD feeds a very large number of circuits, especially in an area laden with dust or subject to damp conditions, nuisance tripping may occur.

In this situation, an RCD with a higher tripping threshold of 100mA could be considered. The reader may understandably question the purpose of this, because it would give little protection against electric shock, but it is here that the RCD's other purpose surfaces.

A device with a small earth leakage fault may be in the early stages of a much more serious fault current, which may develop gradually, and result in a fire, well before the current is sufficient to trip the circuit breaker (or fuse) protecting it. In this situation, an RCD that detects a much lower current value to earth, even at 100mA, would disconnect the faulty device very much earlier than a circuit breaker and even earlier than a fuse. The RCD can therefore, under some conditions, disconnect the equipment and reduce the likelihood of a serious electrical fire.

From a 100mA RCD protecting the overall installation, one or more 30mA RCDs can be fed to protect individual circuits that pose the most risk to the individuals, for example, sockets from which handheld tools are fed.

Note: The requirements for installing RCDs vary from country to country and I can only give the briefest detail of the requirements in the UK. However, since completing this book, I have become aware of new regulations, published in 2008, that have made it mandatory for outlet sockets to be protected by an RCD except in a few very special cases. In future, therefore, all sockets fitted in the workshop should be protected in this way. Therefore, all readers, both within and outside the UK, should check the requirements when the workshop is being fitted out.

Installation

Once you have decided on the extent of the electrical installation within the workshop, there remains the question of how to carry this out. In the case of a purpose-built workshop, one option would be to include the cabling within the structure of the building. For a wooden shed, this would be between the outer boarding and the inner lining, and passing through holes in the building's framework.

The advantage of this system is that it produces a tidy result and protects the cabling from any mechanical damage arising from workshop activity. On the other hand, damage can occur during the fitting of shelves, etc. – which is not uncommon, even within a domestic property. Because of this, the latest regulations in the UK specify that such circuits must be protected by an RCD, even if they are supplying circuits other than sockets, such as lighting. This, I feel, makes it a "no-go". Another minus factor is the difficulty involved in changing the installation, either to add or to move power sockets or lighting fittings.

Surface wiring avoids these problems but is open to damage. Personally, I consider it untidy and, because it may not satisfy the regulations, it will need checking.

My preferred method is to create timber trunking around the workshop to carry the cables, with the sockets and switches placed into this at the required locations (see Photos 9 and 10). It should be apparent from the photographs that the timber has a recess along its length, enabling strips of ply to be fixed using spots of contact adhesive at intervals. These can be easily removed if changes are

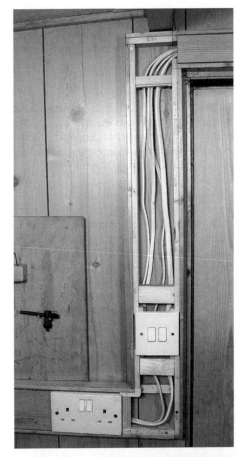

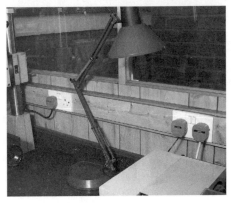

9./10. A method of installing the electrics that is tidy and easy to both install and modify.

deemed necessary. A similar but slightly less tidy approach is to fit surface-mounted sockets and to run the cables between these using plastic trunking. In addition, in a workshop involved in a particularly arduous activity, the use of metal-clad switches and sockets, and even metal conduit to house the cable, is worth considering. However, with this arrangement, it is essential that there is earth continuity throughout the complete installation.

Lighting

This is quite straightforward but I would advise you to be generous with the installation: too much lighting is much better than too little, which may be dangerous. One point that is worth considering is the division of the overhead lighting into two circuits: one adjacent to the windows and one on the opposite side of the workshop. There is then no need to switch on the lighting near the windows during daylight hours.

Heating

On the basis that the heating will be electric, there are three options

- radiators
- fan heaters
- radiant heaters.

Oil-filled radiators are ideal for background heating and you can always turn them up if you intend to spend more than an hour or two in the workshop. Fan heaters are a more rapid means of raising the temperature and are therefore ideal for bringing the workshop up to a comfortable temperature once you start working. As they are likely to raise the temperature rather

quickly, wider air temperature variations are likely and these may cause, rather than prevent, condensation. Therefore, they are not one of the best choices for background heating.

Both the above are floor-standing and, provided a little care is taken in positioning them, they are ideal for use in the workshop. I consider both should be installed and used for the purposes mentioned. Whilst domestic oil-filled radiators may be acceptable, do use an industrial-quality fan-heater.

The case for using radiant heaters is less convincing. They have the advantage of supplying heat almost instantaneously, provided, of course, that you are standing in front of them. Floor-level heaters are available, although I hesitate to recommend one, and you certainly should not moved them around the workshop as you move from machine to machine. However, I do have a wall-mounted one that I find useful when going into the workshop for just half an hour or so. The location is an important consideration and I would suggest that you think carefully about this before installing such a heater.

If you are fortunate enough to have a very large workshop, such as a barn, your fortune stops when it comes to heating it economically. In this case, provided you have adequate floor space, I suggest using use one of the electrical radiant patio heaters that are currently available. This can be moved around to the location where you are working, although, again, you should consider your situation carefully before taking up the idea.

Chapter 4

Planning

Once you have built and fitted out your workshop, you may think it is time to start thinking about tools and machines. However, there are still some considerations to be taken into account, which I refer to as "planning".

Planning can be divided into two areas: general, for the workshop and its eventual projects, and, individually, for each project as it is undertaken. Considering general planning first, probably the most important requirement is to decide which measurement system the workshop should be set up for: metric or imperial. (Here, I am viewing this from a UK perspective.)

Metric or imperial?
If you are setting up a new workshop then I would urge you to opt for metric, whatever the ultimate purpose of the workshop. Although it will be a very long time until imperial measurements disappear (if they ever do), they will eventually be relegated largely to conservation work. However, in the model-engineering arena, existing designs will delay the system's demise, and so I realise that, for some readers, the choice will not be an easy one. Whatever your decision and the workshop's purpose, working with mixed units

1. The regular intervals between the sizes of metric drills make them preferable to imperial drills with their haphazard size intervals.

is inevitable, but with a careful approach this is not as difficult as you may think.

Drill sizes
Even if you choose imperial machines, I would urge you to consider metric in other areas, particularly in your choice of drill sizes. The regular size intervals with metric drills are far more sensible than the haphazard intervals with imperial drills. Typically, if we take a letter

K drill (0.2810in.) and compare this with the next size up, 9/32in. (0.28125in.), it is only 1/4 of one thou. larger. However, the next size up from 9/32in. is letter L, which, at 0.2900in., is almost 9 thou. larger. I would suggest therefore that you purchase the two common metric sets, 1mm to 6mm and 6mm to 10mm, both in 0.1mm (nominally 4 thou.) increments (**Photo 1**).

Thread systems

Not quite as easy a decision is which thread system to use. Again, if you are into model engineering and using early designs, BA thread sizes will be common. However, if you are into other activities, it will be easier to go with the flow and use metric threads, which are rapidly becoming the standard.

Calibrated equipment

Once you have chosen your system of measurement, working to it is not that difficult, even if your machines are calibrated otherwise, as mine are. For this to be the case, however, it is essential that your measuring equipment is calibrated to your chosen system. Fortunately, many measuring devices are calibrated with dual units, for example, rules, vernier callipers and height gauges (**Photo 2**). This mainly leaves micrometers, which you should purchase to conform to your chosen system.

If, like me, you have to work to metric dimensions on imperial machines, the following example will show that it is not that difficult; it just requires a little simple mental arithmetic.

If presented with a diameter of, say, 16mm that needs to be reduced very accurately to 9.50mm, you should never attempt to take off the 3.25mm on radius at one pass; instead you should approach with caution and reduce the diameter in stages:

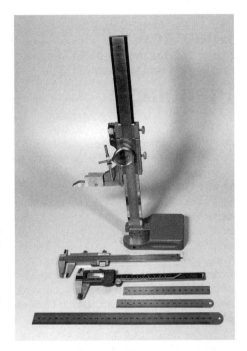

2. This range of tools is calibrated in both metric and imperial units.

1. Working on the basis that 1mm equals 40 thou., one can take a cut of 120 thou. (3mm approximately) to reduce the diameter to around 10mm. If now the diameter reads 9.95mm, then 0.45mm needs removing, that is 0.225mm off the radius.
2. Next, working to approximation that 0.1mm = 4 thou, then this would indicate a cut of 9 thou. However as you need to get very precisely to the value of 9.50mm, remove just 8 thou.
3. Read the dimension again and, finally, working to the approximation that that 0.01mm equals 0.4 thou, make a final pass to arrive at the required diameter.

If you are hesitant about this approach, note

that 0.4 thou. is actually equal to 0.01016mm and error of 0.00016mm (or in imperial terms 0.0000063in., just over six-thousandths of 1 thou.) is, in practical terms, nothing!

Metric measuring equipment

The best approach, therefore, is to equip your workshop with metric measuring equipment even if your machines are imperial. No doubt, in this case, you will also find yourself working to imperial dimensions for some projects, so imperial micrometers will also be useful. An extra micrometer or two will cost only a minute fraction of the overall cost of the workshop, and it will be money well spent in terms of convenience.

In countries where the metric system is predominant, workshop owners will have the same problems, but in reverse, when building to imperial designs. However, the same approach will still be applicable although it will require converting from fractions (1/16in., 1/32in., 1/64in., etc.). They have my sympathies!

Material specifications

It can be very frustrating, and none the less confusing, to find that two similar components machined from separate bars of so-called "mild steel" machine very differently: one well, one quite poorly. The answer, obviously, is that they have different material specifications. Unless you know their specifications, you will be unable to purchase material with the confidence of knowing that is the equal of the one that machines well. The answer, of course, is always to order your materials to a given specification, and to ensure that they are stored in such a way that the information is retained.

Steel

Unfortunately, steel is often listed just as "mild steel", or perhaps "free-cutting mild steel". However, the term "free cutting" is a loose one,

and what is one person's idea of free cutting may not be another's. My advice, therefore, is to purchase materials from a supplier who provides precise details of their specification.

There are, of course, a large number of specifications, designed to suit very special requirements, typically, bending, welding, case-hardening. In these and similar situations, you will need to research the situation in greater depth; a good supplier should be able to advise you.

General-purpose steel

The majority of the materials that you purchase will be for general-purpose components, either turned or milled. Ideally, super free-cutting materials will machine best with both processes. Unfortunately, although super free-cutting material is widely available in rounds, hexagons and squares, predominantly for use on the lathe, rectangular material, which would mostly be used on the milling machine, is available in only a limited range of sizes.

Lead content

For turning, I would therefore strongly recommend using 230M07 steel. If you wish to use the ultimate in free-cutting steel, you could use a version of this that has a small lead content. This is known as 230M07Pb but is available in only a limited range of sizes. However, except for squares, which appear to be limited, rounds and hexagons are available in all the sizes likely to be needed in the home workshop.

Where possible, 230M07 should also be used for components that require machining on the milling machine. The range of sizes of rectangular bar, although limited, is probably sufficient for most home workshop applications but is unfortunately not widely stocked.

If a size is not available in 230M07, then 070M20 is a reasonable alternative and is available in a wide range of sizes and in all the common shapes. Another specification often offered, and in a similar range of shapes and sizes is 080A15. Both of these specifications machine similarly but less well than 230M07.

Steel to 070M20 is suitable for welding, as is 080A15, but the latter is preferable for case hardening.

As an indication of the machinability of the various types of steel, the following is an extract from a much longer list, where 100 is based on 230M07, with numbers above 100 machining better than the ones below.

3. The end of a steel bar stamped 1A L, indicating that its specification is EN1A leaded.

230M07Pb	130
230M07	100
070M20	55
080A15	55
080M40	44
303S42	52

The six-digit specification numbers are used internationally so they should still be quoted in the standards of countries other than the UK.

Unfortunately, many suppliers still list their materials using the earlier EN system. In many cases they are almost, but not exactly, equivalent. The six-digit numbers with their nearest EN steel equivalents are listed below.

230M07Pb	EN1APb
230M07	EN1A
070M20	EN3B
080A15	No EN alternative
080M40	EN8
303S42	EN58A.

The benefits of purchasing material to a known specification will be lost if you then lose track of the specification. Whilst I work to the latest six-digit references, I also stamp both ends of each bar with the reference 1A, 3B, etc. (Photo 3). In this way, if I cut a piece from the bar and forget to re-stamp it, I still have the reference on one end. I still have materials dating from the days before I became particular regarding my material stock; these are stamped P (poor), F (fair) and G (good), as my experience using them indicates. In fact, some were so poor compared to those I now purchase that I consigned them to the scrap bin.

Non-ferrous metals
You should adopt the same basic principle (i.e. to purchase materials of a known specification) when purchasing other materials, such as aluminium and brass. The following are freely available from suppliers to the home workshop and should be a good starting point when you are considering a suitable metal to use. Within their type, both are free machining.

Aluminium 6082 (formerly BS HE30)
Brass CZ121

Project planning

I have read that there is not the pressure in the home workshop to get a part made in the shortest possible time, unlike in a commercial operation, where even saving a few seconds is important. Even so, most workshop owners will agree that there is insufficient time to carry out all the tasks that they would like to do. This all adds up to the need to work efficiently in order to achieve the best possible result within the time available. Good planning at the initial stage of a project is essential if this aim is to be achieved.

Study the drawings

If the project has been designed by someone else and all the drawings are available, so you do not need to draw them yourself, there will be areas that you will not immediately understand. The first stage is to study them thoroughly. This can be carried out in the comfort of your home, which is a pleasant feature of this activity, particularly if the project has a midwinter starting date!

First, you must work out how the parts fit together and, if it is a mechanism, how it will function. At this stage, there is no need to consider the dimensions, just how the parts are assembled. You should also check that there is a part drawing for each component of the assembly, because it is not unknown for one to be missing.

Tolerances

Once you have worked out how the parts fit together, the next stage is to decide what effect this will have on the parts when they are machined. The question of tolerances crops up from time to time, with workshop owners questioning why they are not included on the

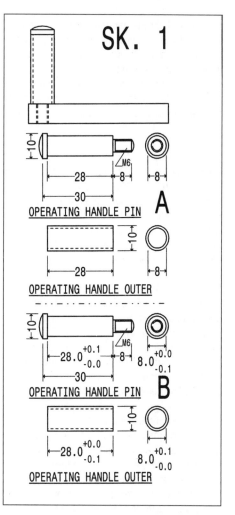

published drawings. As a simple example, consider the parts that make up the component in Sk. 1A.

This sketch shows a handle for a leadscrew in which the outer tube is required to rotate on the inner pin in order to make the leadscrew easy to turn. For the assembly to work, the length of the tube should be just shorter than the parallel portion of the pin, and the hole in the tube should be slightly larger than the pin's diameter. This could be covered on the drawings by the inclusion of tolerances, as in Sk. 1B. However, if, for example, you have made the outer tube first and found it to be a little on the short side, it would be foolish to throw it away and attempt to make another according to the drawing. The answer is to make the pin slightly shorter to match.

Tolerances are mainly intended to be applied to the batch production of assemblies where two complementary parts are made in quantity and in isolation from one other. This sketch shows you how to interpret the dimensions on the drawings so that the parts function satisfactorily when assembled.

The next stage is to study each individual part in detail, making sure that you understand the dimensions given and how they relate to the part to be made. Whilst I would not suggest that you check the drawings in depth, do look out for any obvious errors or, more likely, omissions. If you do find a few errors then it is sensible to make a more thorough check.

Listing your materials
Next, list the materials required and check them against the sizes you already have available. This will probably entail a visit to the workshop. Then place an order for any items that you still need so that everything will be available when you start. A similar approach should be taken regarding hardware, nuts, screws, etc., as well as required tools, typically taps and dies. It is also a good idea to take copies of the drawings for use in the workshop, so that you can add notes, calculations, changes, etc. without defacing the originals.

Saving time
A full understanding of the drawings and their purpose will avoid confusion and delay during the manufacturing stages, but there is still room for saving some man-hours.

Working in parallel
It may seem logical to work on one part at a time, from start to completion, before starting work on another. However, time savings can be made by working on parts in parallel. A simple example is the initial preparation of materials. Look out for parts made from the same sized material and cut lengths to suit each of them at the same time. This is better than cutting off one length, re-marking the bar with its specification and returning it to stock, only to find later that you need another length – and possibly, later still, even another!

Tool changes
Another tip is to avoid unnecessary tool changes, typically from three to four jaw chucks and back again, or from vices to angle plates, etc. If you have just part machined an item in the vice, look out for other parts that may need the same treatment before changing to the angle plate in order to continue machining the part that you have just started.

Drawings
Even if you are preparing to make something to your own design, most of the above will still apply. However, if you are working to your own drawings, the "getting-to-know" process will not be necessary. That is, of course, if you have produced any drawings! In the early days, I have myself been guilty of attempting to design equipment "on the job", so to speak, and am very aware that this is far from satisfactory. For all but the simplest item, you should make some attempt to produce assembly and part drawings, even if they are only freehand.

An improvement on this would be to draw the designs manually using a drawing board and T-square. This need not involve anything

4. A simple drawing board for workshop use.

elaborate; the set-up in Photo 4 is more than adequate for relatively simple items. Indeed, this took me no more than half-an-hour to make and is one of the most useful items in my workshop. As it can also be used horizontally, it makes a useful raised bench for carrying out a wide range of activities (such as marking out, delicate assembly work, soldering electronic assemblies, etc.), and being raised improves visibility. However, it was initially made to hold sheet metal for cutting with a jigsaw or nibbler, a task that it performs well because it is easy to clamp the sheet firmly in place (Photo 5). This is not obvious from the photographs but, in both cases, it is mounted in the bench vice.

Computer-aided design (CAD)

If you have access to a computer, then I strongly advise you to install a computer-aided design (CAD) program. Although these can be very expensive, there are also quite good packages that can be had free or for just a few tens of pounds. A major advantage of CAD is the ease with which changes can be made, especially during the design stages, but also when drawing the detail parts. (For further details about CAD, see Chapter 8.)

If you are producing your own design, with fully detailed drawings, your involvement need not stop at just making the item. You could also have the added satisfaction of producing an article for publication in one of the workshop magazines.

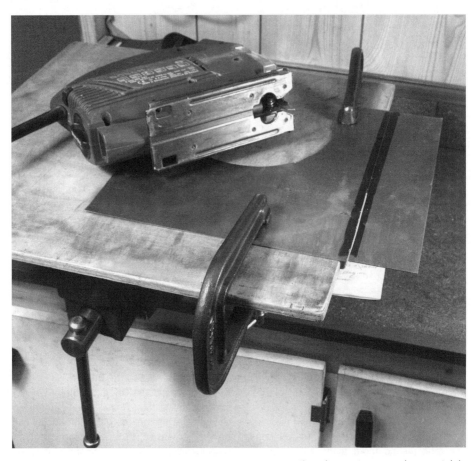

5. The drawing board can be used for other tasks if it is mounted horizontally. In this case, it is being used to hold a piece of sheet steel for cutting, a task for which the board was originally made. Notice how it is mounted in the bench vice, as it would be when used as a drawing board.

Completing the project

Another very important aspect of planning when considering a major project is to ask yourself whether you have sufficient finance, time, and patience to complete the task. More years ago than I care to remember, certainly well before the days of Yamahas and the like, I considered making an electronic organ. During my investigations I read an article warning that there were almost certainly more unfinished than finished instruments. This warning had the desired effect and I shelved the project before starting. As I well know, there are quite a few unfinished metalworking projects around, so please do not add one of your own to the list.

Chapter 5

Hand tools

Hand tools come in a very wide range, some very common and used in other disciplines, typically DIY, and others more specialised and used predominantly in the metalworking workshop. Some files come in such a wide variety of types and sizes that it is impossible to cover the subject fully in this book. Others, such as hammers, pliers, screwdrivers, are so common and well known that they do not merit discussion.

Files

The range of files needed in the home workshop depends on the tasks to be undertaken. In addition, for many tasks, they have now been superseded by milling machines, belt and disk sanders, etc. My advice therefore is to purchase a basic selection and add to it as needs dictate.

Their lengths come in 2in. increments, ranging from 4in. to 14in. or even longer. I suggest purchasing two lengths to start with: either 4in. and 8in., or 6in. and 10in., depending on the nature of the work that you wish to undertake. In my opinion, any file longer than 10in. will only find minimal use in the average set-up. The six most common (**Photo 1**) are:

1. The six most common file types (from left to right): hand, half round, flat, three square (triangular), round and square.

- hand files, which have parallel sides but are very slightly tapered on the thickness. These have one safe (uncut) edge, allowing the file to be used into a corner without filing one of the surfaces.
- flat files, which are similar, but the width is tapered on about the end third and both edges having a cutting face.
- half round files, with one flat face and one round face that meet at the edge, so there

are no side faces. The end third of the file is tapered both in width and thickness.

- round, square and three square (triangular) files, which differ in cross-section but are all similar in shape, i.e. tapered towards the outer end.

As hand and flat files are similar, there is no need to purchase both, so I would recommend the hand file because it has a safe edge. On that basis, I consider that one of each type, apart from the flat file, should make up the workshop's starter set.

Files also come in three tooth sizes: bastard (coarse), second cut and fine cut. Again, I can only say that choice will depend on use. However, I suggest that you choose either bastard or second cut for your longer files and second cut or fine cut for your shorter ones, on the basis that the larger the file the more likely that you will use it aggressively.

In addition to coarseness, there is one other aspect of the cut that is not always mentioned in suppliers' catalogues, namely single cut or double cut. With single cut, the cutting edge is produced at an angle to the side of the file whereas, with double cut, a second cutting edge is made at a similar angle but from the other edge (**Sk. 1**), which produces a diamond pattern. The double cut is by far the most common and is becoming the standard, which may be why the single cut is seldom mentioned.

Other lengths and shapes, and finer and coarser cuts, are also available but the fact that they do not appear in the majority of the catalogues is an indication of their limited use.

However, one other common type of file has yet to be mentioned, and that is the needle file. These very small files have a built-in handle and are made in a wide range of cross-sections

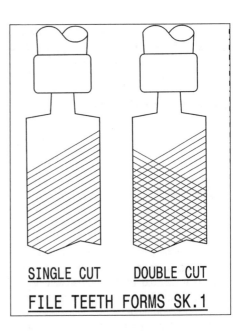

SINGLE CUT   DOUBLE CUT

FILE TEETH FORMS SK.1

2. Needle files are essential for detailed intricate detailed work.

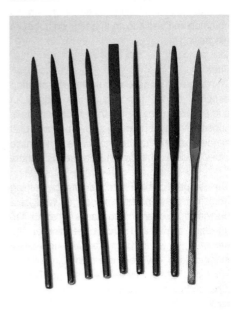

and in three cuts, known as 0, 2 and 4 (**Photo 2**). These are essential for finely detailed work, such as modelling in the smallest scales or making small-size clocks.

Using a file correctly is most definitely a skill that can only be achieved with practice, and I suggest that you seek further information on the process and the types of file available.

Scrapers

Scrapers, like files, are tools for removing metal from the surface of a workpiece. However, the comparison ends there, because the file is intended to remove rather more than the scraper. Scrapers are normally available in three forms: curved, flat and triangular (**Photo 3**). Apart from the triangular scrapers use for deburring holes, the flat scraper is probably the most used.

The most usual method of using a scraper is to highlight the raised portions of the workpiece, then use the scaper to remove small amounts of metal at this point. To do this, an accurately flat (or mating curved) surface is needed to act as a comparison. This can be either a surface plate (see Chapter 6) or a reasonable substitute, such as a piece of plate glass. The reference surface is smeared very lightly with engineer's marking blue and the workpiece is then placed on it and moved slightly in a figure-of-eight motion. This process will leave small blue patches on the high spots of the workpiece which can then removed using the scraper. As the process is repeated, the number and size of the blue patches will increase until they are closely packed over the entire surface. Provided there are no large areas without a blue covering, the result should be adequate for most applications. If you have time, you can always attempt to improve the coverage.

This process is typically used to produce a surface plate or to finalise the fit of machine

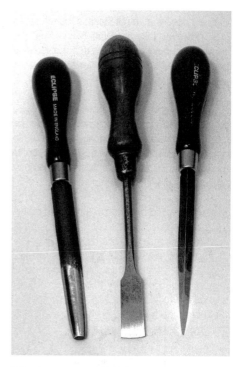

3. Hand scrapers: curved (left), flat (centre) and triangular (right).

slides. In the latter case, the very shallow hollows produced by the process will provide pockets that will retain oil and lubricate the slide.

Large bronze or white metal bearings can be scraped in a similar manner, to match the bearing to the spindle with which they are to be used. The flat surface would normally be scraped using a flat scraper and the bearing using a half round scraper. A three square (triangular) scraper could be used for scraping the narrow faces of the dovetails on a machine slide, but it is normally used for deburring holes.

The three commercially available scrapers shown in **Photo 3** can be made quite easily from old files that have passed their use-by date. However, take care not to overheat the file when grinding away the teeth and creating the required shape or it will lose its required hardness.

Because of the very small depth of metal to be removed, the end of the flat scraper must be kept totally sharp; it is physically impossible to remove, say, 0.001mm if the edge has a radius of 0.002mm. The edge must therefore be near-perfect!

Sharpening a scraper is a job for the flat stone.

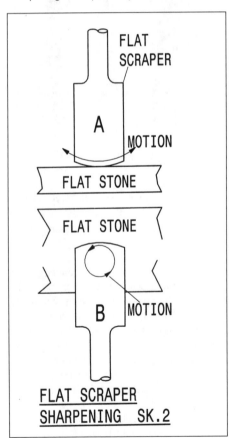

FLAT SCRAPER

A MOTION

FLAT STONE

FLAT STONE

B MOTION

FLAT SCRAPER
SHARPENING SK.2

It can be ground very lightly on an off-hand grinder to re-establish the curved end but the end should be polished on a fine flat stone, as illustrated in **Sk. 2A**. Do this on a fairly hard stone as the narrow end will tend to cut a groove in it. Once you have polished the end, polish the sides using a relatively fine stone, say 1000 grit minimum (**Sk. 2B**).

Spanners

In day-to-day terms, spanners are of limited use in the average home workshop unless you are into the restoration of vintage cars, or do your own maintenance on the modern equivalent.

The home workshop should be equipped with the very best spanners in the sizes that get the most frequent use, for items such as the clamping nuts used on the machine tables and the top of the milling machine's draw bar and, in the case of smaller sizes, for clamping on the lathe's faceplate. In terms of safety, it is advisable to have ring spanners as well as open-ended spanners.

Hexagon wrenches

If kept in good order these have a lot going in their favour as they are more secure having the same benefits as a ring spanner. You may be tempted to purchase a set of short wrenches or, even more likely, to make do with those supplied free with every conceivable item purchased. Don't do this. Instead, purchase a set of long-reach, ball-ended wrenches (Photos 4 & 5).This will be money well spent because the long reach and, in particular, the ball end makes working on inaccessible cap head screws so much easier than with standard wrenches. For screws in inaccessible places, it is well worth taking a short length from a standard wrench and driving it into a length of bar (**Photo 4, centre**).

At the simpler end of the range, there are items such as rules, centre punches, scribers, etc. These require little comment because they are generally very commonplace and without complication. For the rules, I would suggest a flexible 150mm rule and a rigid 300mm rule, preferably in satin chrome because this makes them so much easier to read.

Centre punches
It is worth having two centre punches, one sharpened to a 90° point and the other to a 30–45° point. The sharper one will locate more

6. Centre punches: standard (left) and spotting punch (right)

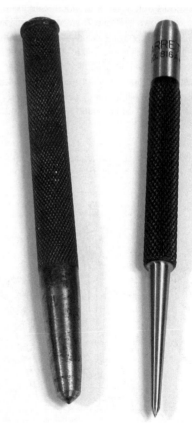

4./5. Ball-ended hexagon wrenches (Photo ?) are much easier to use than the normal type (Photo ?), especially in difficult locations.

Measuring and marking-out tools
This is a vast subject, and an area that requires a much greater level of financial commitment as far as hand tools are concerned.

easily in the scribed lines and, with a light tap from the hammer, can be used to produce a small indent in readiness to use the 90° point to produce the working indent. The sharper punches are often known as "spotting" or "prick" punches and can be ground from a standard centre punch (**Photo 6, left**). In addition to locating in the scribed lines more easily, the sharper angle makes it easier to view the point to be punched. Viewing can be further enhanced by purchasing a special spotting punch that has a smaller diameter shank than normal (**Photo 6, right**).

Callipers and dividers

Three tools that have been much used in the past are shown in Photo 7: an outside calliper (left), divider (centre) and inside calliper (right). Whether you will find a use for the callipers depends on the sophistication of your other measuring equipment (micrometers, etc.), but I suspect they will be rarely used. The divider, however, which can be used for marking out

circles and stepping along lines and around circles in equal increments, is a tool worthy of any workshop

Depth gauge/Protractor

You will rarely need to work with angles other than 90°. However, it is inevitable that, at some time, you will require some means of measuring or setting out angles. There is a range of equipment available for this, varying in price from a few pounds to more than a hundred pounds. In most cases, there will be no great demand for accuracy, and a depth gauge/protractor (**Photo 8**, front) will be more than adequate and may suit all your requirements. For much greater accuracy, you will need a universal bevel protractor (**Photo 8**, rear). Whilst the depth gauge will work to, say, 0.5°, the universal bevel will work to 0.1°, or even better.

Combination square set

In terms of accuracy, the combination square set (**Photo 9**) falls between the two. Its accuracy is comparable to that of the depth gauge/protractor but its more robust build makes it suitable for a greater number of applications. It also has extra facilities that make it a good proposition, such as a centre-finding square

7. Outside calliper (left), divider (centre) and inside calliper (right). In most cases, only the divider is an essential workshop item.

8. A depth gauge/protractor (front) and a universal bevel protractor (rear).

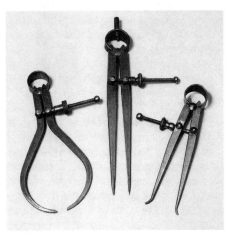

9. Combination square sets with centre-finding square (left) and conventional square (right).

(**Photo 9,** left) and a conventional square (**Photo 9,** right). The rule also doubles as a good-quality 300mm rule. Both the protractor and the square include a spirit level and, provided that you have set your machine tables level, this can help you to set components at an angle for machining. This will not be precise but will be adequate for many applications.

Combination square sets are made in qualities ranging from those made from die castings, appropriate only for DIY use, to high-quality versions suitable for use in an industrial tool room. Something between the two will be appropriate for use in the home workshop. My advice would be to purchase a mid-quality combination set in preference to the other two items mentioned above.

Another method of setting out angles is to use a sine bar (see Chapter 6), but whilst this is capable of producing very accurate results, the applications where it can easily be used are very limited.

Getting back to setting and checking for an angle of 90°, I suggest that you purchase two squares: one small, say 50mm, and a larger one of 150mm blade length. The larger will often be too large for intricate set-ups and the smaller much too small for the majority of situations.

Marking out

There are many instances when it is necessary to mark out a part for machining, although I feel three are the most common. Starting with the most common, these are:

1. marking out hole positions for drilling
2. marking out a part for sawing – this may be just for cutting a length from a bar or for shaping a component using a band saw or hand-held jig saw
3. marking out machining lines on a part before placing it on the machine table.

The third, I feel, is not used as much as it should be. It is much easier than attempting to measure the part in situ on the table during the machining process, where, access and the presence of pieces of swarf can make it difficult. A typical example for this is marking out the ends and width of a closed end slot to be machined using a slot drill, a situation

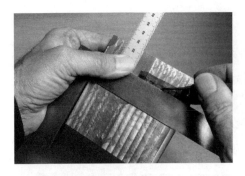

10. Marking out with a hand-held square

With this done, a line is scribed (**Photo 10**); for drilling a hole, a second line will be necessary at 90° to the first.

In some cases, depending on factors such as surface finish and lighting level, scribed lines can be difficult to see. This can be overcome by covering the area to be marked out with a film of engineer's marking blue. A present-day and easier to use alternative is a wide-nibbed felt-tipped marker. Any dark colour will do, but stay with tradition and use blue. Photo 11 shows this, together with the other tools required for marking out by this method.

An alternative to the square and rule method is to use the device shown in Photo 12. This is very clearly marked in millimetres and can easily be set to better than a millimetre, certainly 0.5mm. The wide locating and scribing faces can be easily set, making it very easy to use, and it is adequate for a wide range of marking-out requirements.

where high precision is rarely called for. Of course, some cases do require precision and the only option is to measure the part while it is on the machine table, although machining lines can still be made as an initial indication of the machine-to position.

Once you have decided that a part needs to be marked out for later operations, you have a choice of two methods. The hand-held approach consists, basically, of using an engineer's square off of one edge and measuring its required distance from another.

11. Tools required for marking out. The broad-nibbed felt-tipped pen in the foreground is a modern alternative to engineer's marking blue.

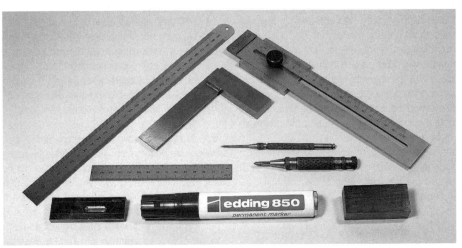

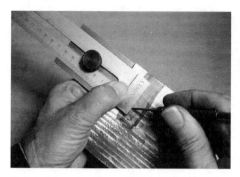

12. An excellent alternative to using a hand-held square for marking out.

13. Using a surface plate and surface gauge for marking out. Where complex shapes are involved this is the only practical method.

Where greater accuracy is required than is achievable with the above methods, it will be necessary to use a surface plate, together with various additional items. However, whilst very little more accurate than the above methods, using a surface gauge (**Photo 13**) is frequently the easier option, sometimes where others are not possible. A surface gauge is therefore an essential item, unless a height gauge is to be purchased. This, together with surface plates, is discussed in Chapter 6.

Hand stamps

This is a quite different method of marking and has a different purpose. Like much else in this book, whether hand stamps will have a purpose in your workshop depends on the purpose of the workshop. Nonetheless, even if you only use them to stamp an identification reference on the ends of material stock, it is worth acquiring a set.

Hand stamps are commonly available in sizes ranging from 1.5mm to 6mm, but smaller and larger sizes are also available. Choose the size very carefully as, in my experience, the end result may be larger than anticipated. Stamps at the budget end of the price range should suit as they work quite well.

Hand-stamping entirely free hand is likely to produce a visually poor result: out of line and unevenly spaced. This may not be much of a problem, say for a plant label for the garden, but will often be unacceptable. Because of this, you will need to produce some simple device for guiding them. In addition, using a guide makes it easier to return the punch to the same place should you decide that a deeper impression would be preferable.

Chapter 6

Precision tools

A very wide range of tools fits into the classification of precision tooling, many of which are essential items. I have also included others for academic interest and because, while they are not appropriate in the vast majority of workshops, the newcomer may come across them and wonder whether to acquire them.

Micrometers

Outside micrometers come in a surprising range of types, but fortunately almost all are very specialised and definitely beyond the requirement of the home workshop. However, the basic outside-diameter micrometer is essential and the only decisions relate to the type of units, range and quality.

The units that you have chosen, metric or imperial, will determine which micrometer, or micrometers, to obtain. Obviously starting at the smallest 0–25mm (or 0–1in.), you then need to decide which larger sizes, if any, you may need. Whatever the workshop's purpose, I firmly believe that 25–50mm, or the imperial equivalent, should also be obtained (Photo 1) and, at these sizes, do purchase the best possible because they will get a lot of use on occasions when accuracy is most vital.

1. 0–25 and 25–50mm micrometers. Both are essential in most workshops.

If you anticipate working in both metric and imperial units on a frequent basis, you should purchase micrometers in both units, certainly in the smaller sizes. Converting metric units so that they can be measured on tooling intended for imperial units, and vice versa, should be limited to the occasional requirement.

In addition to outside micrometers, there is a wide range of micrometers for other purposes; the two most likely to find a use are for taking depth and inside measurements.

Depth micrometers are available that only measure 0–25mm, but most have interchangeable spindles so they can be used over a wider range, typically 0–100mm (**Photo 2**). The spindles are

2. 0-100mm depth micrometer with interchangeable spindles.

smaller than those on outside micrometers, in the order of 4mm diameter, enabling them to measure into narrow grooves. They can, of course, also measure steps, etc. As they probably get much less use than outside micrometers, it may be acceptable to obtain just a single micrometer and use it for both units of measurement.

Micrometers for measuring internal dimensions, (**Photo 3**) will most probably be used to measure internal diameters, typically bores being turned on the lathe, but they can also

3. Inside micrometers are also very useful. These are 5–30mm and 25–50mm sizes. The disks shown are for calibrating the micrometers and are included with the purchase.

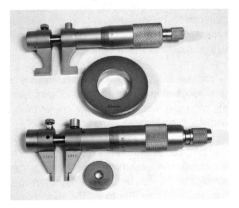

be used for measuring widths of slots, etc. Obviously, the smallest, which has a range of 5–30mm, cannot measure from zero. Larger sizes, however, revert to the normal ranges: 25–50mm, etc. Again, a single micrometer may be acceptable for both units of measurement.

Inside micrometers that go completely into the hole or slot are also available. These have interchangeable spindles, rather like depth micrometers, to extend their range, and a very large span of sizes is available. At the lower end, a typical set would measure between 50mm and 200mm. I would not suggest that micrometers in this range are anywhere near essential, although those up to 50mm, as shown in Photo 3, can be very useful, probably more so than the depth micrometer.

A rather specialised micrometer is the multi-anvil unit shown in Photo 4. Whilst this can in no way be considered essential, its various uses may swing the balance in its favour if you can afford it. It can be fitted with a small diameter rod anvil, allowing it to be used, for example, for measuring the wall thickness of a tube. Similarly, it can measure from the edge of a hole to the side of a component.

The rod anvil can be replaced with a thin flat anvil, enabling the micrometer to measure from a thin groove. This is particularly useful

4. A multi-anvil micrometer.

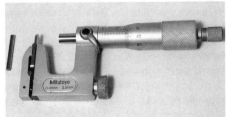

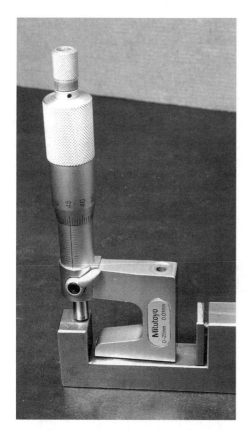

5. With the anvils removed, the micrometer can be used for measuring steps.

because a normal outside micrometer is likely to start at a groove width of around 10mm. The rod anvil will be in the order of 3mm diameter, whereas the flat anvil is about 1.6mm thick. With neither anvil fitted, the micrometer can be used to measure steps (**Photo 5**).

Other micrometers, of which there are very many, are too specialised to warrant inclusion. If you wish to research the subject, get an engineering tools catalogue from a large stockist who supplies to industry. You will probably be amazed at the variety on offer!

Vernier callipers

For many years, vernier callipers (**Photo 6**) have been the alternative to micrometers, particularly for the larger dimensions. For smaller diameters, say up to 50mm, they are no real alternative because they are not so easy to use, and the results will therefore not be as certain. However, they do have the major advantage of being able to read inside, depth and step dimensions in addition to outside diameters (**Sk. 1**), and I would recommend the purchase of the 0–150mm size to provide facilities for measuring larger dimensions. These callipers are one item that is invariably calibrated in both metric and imperial units, and they are therefore a useful back up for the workshop that only occasionally moves from one system of units to the other.

For readers who are not conversant with this method of measurement, a description of the principle, illustrated by Sk. 2, follows.

The main scale is calibrated accurately along the full length of the calliper, but the moving portion is engraved with a limited number of lines only. These are spaced at intervals less than the divisions on the main scale. To simplify the description, I have used whole millimeters, although the vernier will actually be calibrated in much smaller increments.

6. For many years, the vernier calliper has been the normal method of measuring larger dimensions, say 50mm plus, but it has largely been replaced by its digital counterpart.

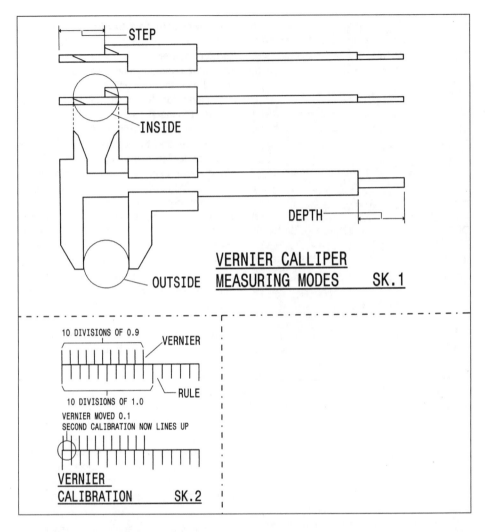

STEP

INSIDE

DEPTH

VERNIER CALLIPER
MEASURING MODES   SK.1

OUTSIDE

10 DIVISIONS OF 0.9

VERNIER

RULE

10 DIVISIONS OF 1.0

VERNIER MOVED 0.1
SECOND CALIBRATION NOW LINES UP

VERNIER
CALIBRATION   SK.2

Assuming that the main rule is calibrated in 1mm increments, then the moving jaw would be calibrated in 0.9mm increments. Starting from zero, both zero lines would line up. However, the next calibration on the moving jaw would be just 0.1mm short of the next calibration on the main scale. To make the next two lines line up, a jaw movement of only 0.1mm is required. The jaw opening will therefore be 0.1mm. By this method, even though the rule is calibrated in 1mm divisions, measurements of 0.1mm can be achieved. In fact, vernier callipers will measure in increments of 0.02mm (0.001in.)

Height gauges
These gauges (**Photo 7**) also function using a vernier scale, enabling them to be set in increments of 0.02mm (0.001in.) The most

common height is 300mm, although shorter ones are sometimes available. A shorter one is likely to be adequate for most workshops and, where this is not the case, the 300mm gauge should suit.

On some height gauges, the main scale is adjustable, up and down, by a small amount, so that all dimensions can be about some point other than the surface plate on which it stands. In my opinion, this facility is of little use in the average workshop so a gauge without the adjustment will be more than adequate.

Dial-type measuring instruments
These come in two types, dial gauges and dial test indicators (often referred to as DTIs).

Dial gauges
Dial gauges (**Photo 8**, left) have a plunger that, when pressed, causes the dial to rotate. Typically, the range is in the order of 12mm and reads in increments of 0.01mm. However, dials with a greater range are available, as are some with a smaller range and calibrated in much smaller increments, typically 0.001mm. The dial can be rotated, enabling it to be zeroed at any convenient point. However, as the pointer will rotate a number of times to cover the travel, a small secondary dial is provided to indicate the number of turns made. Unfortunately, this cannot be zeroed. They are mounted via the barrel through which the plunger works or by using a lug on the rear.

Dial test indicators
Dial test indicators (**Photo 8**, right) work quite differently to dial gauges, making the measurement using a pivoted arm, often referred to as a stylus. They also have a much smaller range and, as a result, their main purpose is as a comparator. In the workshop, the most likely usage is when setting a part to run true in the 4-jaw chuck (**Photo 9**) or to accurately position a vice or workpiece in line with the axis of the table on the milling machine (**Photo 10**).

7. A height gauge is able to very accurately mark out and measure items on the surface plate.

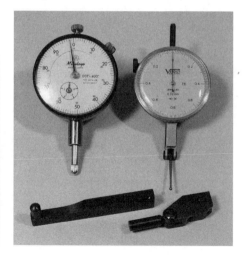

8. Dial indicator (left) and dial test indicator (right), plus mounting accessories

Dial sizes are normally smaller, commonly with a diameter of just 27mm, although larger dials are available. As the indicator has a nominal range of just one revolution, a secondary dial to count turns is not required. Typically, the dial will cover a range of 0.8mm, with the dial calibrated 40-0-40 in 0.01mm increments. As with the dial gauge, the dial can be rotated so that it can be zeroed for easy reading. Although I stated above that they have a nominal range of one revolution, in practice there will be some overrun at each end, but this will normally be less than two turns.

The stylus has a friction mounting at its pivot that enables it to be rotated into the best position for the task in hand. This should be obvious by comparing **Photo 9** and **Photo 10.** In addition, there is a small lever that enables you to change the direction of rotation of the stylus from clockwise to anticlockwise.

Whilst the longer measuring range of the dial gauge may be considered an advantage, the flexibility of the DTI, enabling it to make tests in the most difficult locations, makes it the

10. A DTI can ensure a workpiece is parallel with the milling machine's table traverse.

9. A DTI being used to ensure a component is running true in a 4-jaw chuck.

number one choice. However, there will be a few occasions where the greater range of the dial gauge will be beneficial, so I would wait and see how the workshop's activities develop before purchasing one.

Both types of indicator require a range of accessories to enable them to be mounted for use (see Chapter 10). A typical set-up is shown in **Photo 9.**

Digital versions
Micrometers, vernier callipers, height gauges and dial gauges are all now available in digital versions, but whether you consider these worth

purchasing will depend on your point of view. For me, the benefit of a digital micrometer is minimal because the mechanical version is easy to read, but the situation with regard to a digital calliper is quite different. Vernier callipers are not that easy to read and the convenience of a digital read-out is a definite plus. Therefore, despite its disadvantages (e.g. reliability), I feel that a digital calliper is a must for most workshops.

As digital height gauges are still expensive and are of limited use, I recommend that, if required, you purchase a vernier type. However, the cost will no doubt continue to fall, as it has done with the digital calliper.

Digital dial gauges are also now available and, being digital, do not have the problem of counting turns because the total reading is indicated at all times. I have also seen a digital DTI but, as this is normally used for comparative tests, the analogue meter wins hands down for me.

Electronic devices are covered in a little more detail in the Chapter 7.

Slip gauges
In theory, slip gauges can be very useful in the workshop for measuring distances, setting up table stops, etc. For example, if you are using a lathe to bore a hole to a depth of, say, 17.5mm, then a pack of gauges to a size of 17.5 will enable you to set the saddle stop to this dimension easily. However, they are made to a level of accuracy very much greater than the average home workshop requires, and therefore have a correspondingly high price. This, of course, prices them out of the market for the vast majority of workshops. (In Chapter 7, I suggest an alternative that I refer to as "distance gauges".)

11. A set of imperial slip gauges.

To complete the picture, though purely out of interest for the majority, slip gauges are made in sets of 87 metric blocks or 81 imperial blocks (Photo 11). A metric set permits increments of 0.001mm and an imperial set permits increments of 0.0001in. In the metric set, the smallest block is 1.001mm and the largest 100.000mm. However, some metric sets have an additional block of 1.0005mm, enabling increments of 0.0005mm to be set up. Imperial sets range from 0.1001in. to 4.0000in.

Smaller sets are available: 47 blocks metric and 41 blocks imperial. These have the same range of blocks (i.e. the same maximum and minimum) but fewer in-between sizes. Even so, they can still achieve all the possible sizes

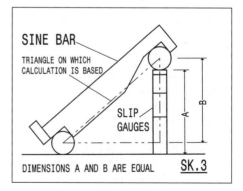

SINE BAR

TRIANGLE ON WHICH
CALCULATION IS BASED

SLIP
GAUGES

A

B

DIMENSIONS A AND B ARE EQUAL   SK.3

within the range, but are limited if you need to set up two or more stacks at the same time, with either the same or different dimensions.

Sine bars

A sine bar's purpose is to accurately set up angles, but this is another item capable of greater precision than the average workshop demands. Even more important, for most applications, the angle is not presented in an easy-to-use fashion; this is best understood by studying at Sk. 3. In addition, they will not function up to a full 90°. This item is unlikely to find much use in the home workshop, and I have included this detail for completeness, not to suggest that the reader should purchase one – rather the reverse!

Hole gauges

Not strictly precision items in themselves, hole gauges (**Photo 12**) are devices very much involved in achieving a precise result. At the smaller sizes, say up to 30mm, the internal micrometers discussed above are a more practical proposition. This is unlikely to apply to the larger sizes, because of their limited use, in which case, it is worth considering a telescopic gauge (Photo 12, left).

To use a telescopic gauge, the two arms of the T, which are spring-loaded, are pushed into the body of the gauge and held in place using a locking mechanism. They are then placed in the hole and unlocked, allowing them to spring out to the hole's diameter, and then locked again. The gauge is then removed and the distance across the arm's ends is measured using an outside micrometer or a vernier calliper. The set shown in the photograph covers the range 12.5–150mm.

The other gauges shown (**Photo 12**, right) operate quite differently. These have a ball end that is split, enabling it to expand to the size of

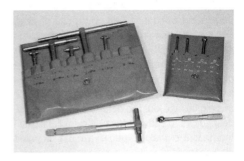

12. Hole gauges: telescopic gauge, up to 150mm (left) and ball-ended gauge, up to 13mm (right). These gauges are used in conjunction with a micrometer and/or a calliper to measure internal dimensions.

the hole that is being measured as a tapered inner is pulled into it. This is done by turning the end of the handle. The width across the ball is then measured. This set covers the range 3–13mm.

Both types are equally at home for imperial sizes, for width of slots as well as holes.

Precision spirit level

A precision spirit level is often quoted as being necessary for the accurate installation of a centre lathe but, although helpful, it is far from essential, as explained later (Chapter 9). Again, it is included for completeness, rather than being a required item.

Photo 13 shows a shop-made version but typical of those available ready made. It is fitted with the most accurate vial available from the supplier and can easily detect an error of 0.1mm over a length of 1000mm. To put this into perspective, in my builder's level, an error of 1mm in 1000mm results in a hardly perceptible deflection of the bubble – and the level in my engineer's combination set is no better!

13. A shop-made precision level, often quoted as necessary for the initial setting up of a lathe. However, alternative and simpler methods are equally acceptable.

14. Fixed width parallels: precision (left), shop-made (centre) and economy (right).

Parallels

Some items of tooling will find a use in many applications, typically, marking out on the surface plate and positioning workpieces on the milling and drilling machines. However, they are mostly made to an accuracy that puts them into the realm of a precision item, even though this level of accuracy is not always required.

Fixed width parallels

Whilst there are some special types, the most common are fixed width parallels (**Photo 14**). Those shown on the left of the photograph are true precision instruments. In this set, there are just four sizes: 1in. to 1-3/4in. in 1/4in. increments. The two larger sizes are 1/2in. thick and the two smaller sizes are 3/16in. thick, and are therefore thick enough to stand firmly on their edges, but the range of widths is rather limited.

A common requirement for parallels is to pack up a workpiece within a vice so that machining can be carried out above its jaws. Workpiece thicknesses vary, so you will need a range of parallel heights and, if you work with two or more vices of different jaw heights, your need will be even greater.

The parallels shown on the right of the photograph are a readily available budget set of 10 pairs of parallels ranging from 1/2in. to 1-5/8in. The 1/8in. increment means that they will meet the requirement of different workpieces and jaw heights but, on the down side, they are only 1/8in. thick and, as a result, will not stand reliably on their own. When they are being used between the vice jaws, this problem can be overcome by placing a largish diameter compression spring between them, although this is hardly a convenient approach. Another minor disadvantage is their length, which at 6in. is rather on the long side for most home workshop activities.

As an alternative, you may like to make some yourself (**Photo 14**, centre). In this case, you can tailor them to your own requirement, a process that is not at all difficult. Few, if any, of the requirements for parallels will benefit from the accuracy of purchased sets, and something a little less precise will be more than adequate.

The essential requirement for a pair of parallels is invariably not their actual width but the fact that they are parallel and both the same height. This can easily be achieved as follows. Mount two round pillars on an angle plate, say at 75mm centres, and at nominally the same height. Using an end mill, very lightly machine their tops at one pass to produce two narrow flats. These flats will then be parallel to the table's traverse. Clamp two pieces of mild steel strip onto the faceplate, ensuring they are in contact with the posts, and lightly machine

59

along the top edge. Turn over and repeat the process and you will have two lengths of steel, accurately parallel, and both the same width. Repeat the process with other widths of material to produce the number you require. Their actual widths are not important, providing the interval between them is sufficiently small, say about 4mm maximum.

Block parallels

A quite different form of solid parallels is the 1-2-3 blocks, so-called because they are 1in. × 2in. × 3in. in size (**Photo 15**). They have 15 holes in the main face, 5 in the side and 3 in the end, with some being clearance and others threaded. I find these extremely useful and, like other parallels, they are sold in matched pairs. Larger 2-4-6 blocks are also available, as are 25-50-75 metric blocks, although the latter are not that easy to find.

"Wavy" parallels

Another form of parallels is the type known as "wavy". These are made of spring steel and in pairs, with a corrugated form that enables them to stand even though they are made from relatively thin steel. The corrugations of a single parallel can be compressed a little between the jaws of the vice, enabling it to grip thinner workpieces. These are less accurate than other types and are of dubious benefit to the average workshop.

Adjustable parallels

Finally, there are the adjustable parallels. These are made from two tapered halves that slide one on the other, thus increasing or decreasing the distance between the parallel sides. This enables the width to be set to the precise dimension required, where it can be locked. They are normally supplied singly, so you would have to purchase two if you need a pair. The amount of adjustment is quite small and six are required to cover a range of 10–55mm.

15. Parallels of a different type. These are 1-2-3 blocks, so-called because they are 1in. × 2in. × 3in. overall.

***

In terms of equipping a workshop, I consider the solid parallels with a small size increment between sizes, either purchased or shop-made, to be essential. A pair of 1-2-3 blocks would also be very useful. The purchase of other items is probably best left until the need arises.

Surface plates

Commercially available surface plates (**Photo 16**) come in two types – cast iron or granite -and in a wide range of sizes. Granite has some distinct advantages: it is harder wearing and more stable with both time and temperature, and it does not rust. Even so, cast iron plates have been used for many years and are perfectly adequate. Irrespective of size, prices seem to vary quite widely, with granite plates usually, but not always, being the more expensive. It is therefore a good idea to check prices, but this should always be done with quality in mind. In this respect, inspection-grade plates are quite unnecessary, workshop-grade plates being more than adequate.

Sizes start at about 250mm × 300mm, which should be adequate for the majority of

16. Two surface plates. The larger has been rescued from an industrial workshop (possibly sometimes used as an anvil) but is still adequate for home workshop use.

workshops. If you need a larger plate, 300mm × 300mm and 300mm × 450mm are also common.

If you feel that you have no need for such an expensive item, or lack the room to store one, as the larger sizes are heavy, then there is an alternative. A piece of plate glass, say 10mm thick, makes a good alternative as, being much thinner and lighter, it will be easier to store. It will also cost much less. On the down side, it will scratch easily, although this is unlikely to be anything other than a cosmetic problem.

In addition to the surface plate, there are two items of equipment commonly used for marking out: the surface gauge and the height gauge (see above). The surface gauge is not a precision item, but the height gauge is capable of marking out (and measuring) to within 0.02mm (0.001in.) Whilst this level of accuracy is not often required, it is much better than can be achieved with the surface gauge, and the height gauge is much easier to use. This makes it a very worthwhile addition to most workshops.

Whilst some workpieces, typically those with a large footprint, will stand on the surface plate adequately on their own, others will need support. Therefore, a few other items are still needed in order to make the best use of the set-up, namely an angle plate, V blocks and parallels. These items will not create any extra expense because they are all essential for use elsewhere.

The angle plate is used to support thin items that will not stand on their own, often when a plate has to be marked out, typically for drilling a number of holes (**Photo 7** shows an example). Angle plates are discussed in detail in the chapter on milling machine accessories (Chapter 14).

V blocks

These are sold in matched pairs and are available in a large number of forms, sizes and levels of precision. The most basic (**Photo 17**, left) are made in by far the widest range of sizes, with footprints up to 8in. × 4-1/2in., possibly even larger. Precision blocks (**Photo 17**, right) are made in a smaller range of sizes but have the advantage of including a workpiece clamp. They are also invariably made to a higher precision level.

The type of V blocks required will depend on the workshop's purpose. However, for the majority of workshops, a pair of precision blocks will be adequate. If larger blocks are considered

17. Three forms of V block: basic blocks (left) are made in large sizes but are less accurate than the precision ones (right). In the foreground are two shop-made blocks.

18. A large magnetic V block. These are unlikely to find a use in most home workshops.

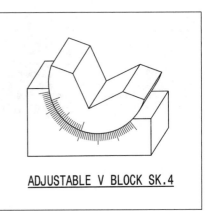

ADJUSTABLE V BLOCK SK.4

necessary, then a pair of basic blocks with a footprint of 4in. × 2in. should suffice. Shop-made blocks are another option (**Photo 17**, foreground).

Magnetic V blocks (**Photo 18**) are also available that hold firm both the workpiece to the V block, and the block to the surface on which it is being used. Their main purpose is for inspection and marking out, but they can also be used for very light machining operations, providing great care is taken. The magnetic grip can be turned on and off and, although they are almost always sold as individual blocks, I have seen a matched pair advertised by one supplier.

Another form of V block is shown in Sk. 4, in which the angle of the V can be varied and to better than 10 minutes (one-sixth of one degree). As with the magnetic V block, I have included this for completeness and do not expect either to find a place in the average home workshop.

Chapter 7

Shop-made tools

No matter what the intended use of their workshop, there will be times when most workshop owners will find it useful to make some items of workshop equipment themselves. This is not to save money, or to provide an interesting project, although it may do both, it is because some very useful items are not available commercially.

Saddle stop
Whenever I have made various items for my workshop and discovered just how useful they are, I have often ask myself why I have done without them for so many years. Number one in this respect is a saddle stop, which took me only an hour or so to make but has saved these hours many times over. More importantly, it has made many operations so much easier, as well as producing a better-quality result. How I wish I had made one when I first established my workshop!

This item is typically used for setting the depth of a blind hole being bored in a workpiece, as shown in **Photo 1**.

A similar situation is boring a through hole in a part mounted on the faceplate. In this case,

1. A saddle stop being used to fix the depth of a hole being bored.

whilst a piece of thin hard card between the workpiece and the faceplate will enable the tool to break through, one lapse of concentration and the tool will contact the faceplate. Using a suitably set saddle stop will prevent this happening. These are but two of the many uses

3./4. For occasional use, simple tapping guides are a good alternative to the tapping stand shown in Photo 2.

2. A tapping stand with controlled feed.

for this device. Some lathe manufacturers may list this item; otherwise, it is a simple task to make one.

Tapping guides

After drilling the appropriate hole, it is still a problem to tap the hole precisely in line with this. Whilst a number designs are available to overcome the problem (see example in Photo 2), there is nothing simpler to make than the tapping guides shown in Photo 3. Photo 4 shows a guide being used, although, for larger thread sizes and/or workpieces, it may need

clamping to the workpiece. The size of the hole is not crucial and I would suggest making it about 0.1mm larger than the tap, with the guide being in the order of 25mm thick.

Universal joints

These are almost as simple to make as the tapping guides above, and although they are available commercially, you may need to approach a supplier to industry to purchase them. They are used for mounting dial indicators, etc. **Photo 5** shows these with a range of associated parts (some not available commercially) while **Photo 6** shows a typical application.

gauges" (my name), providing increments of, say, 0.5mm or perhaps even 0.1mm (**Photo 7**), will find a lot of use.

These gauges are typically used to set the saddle stop (**Photo 8**) for boring a blind hole (as shown in **Photo 1**). In this case, the saddle stop is fitted and a stack of distance gauges made up to the depth of the hole required. These are then placed against the saddle stop and the saddle is moved up to the gauges, thus

7./8. Simple distance gauges being used to set the saddle stop for boring the hole shown Photo 1.

5./6. Dial gauge mounting components and a typical application.

Distance gauges

Slip gauges (see Chapter 6) are unlikely to find a place in the average home workshop because they are far more accurate than is normally required and, as a result, are very expensive. However, a set of shop-made "distance

holding them in place. Using the top slide, the tool is then fed until it just touches the outer face of the item to be bored. Once the gauges have been removed, the bore can be made to the required depth by feeding the saddle. Easy!

Even though I have a set of slip gauges, I make at least 20 times more use of the distance gauges.

Grinding rest

Far too frequently, sharpening workshop tools becomes a task to be carried out totally free hand on the off-hand grinder, and then only when it becomes absolutely necessary. I know this only too well, having been guilty of this

for longer than I care to admit. However, this method is far from ideal and some other should be found. Apart from obtaining a tool and cutter grinder, making an improved rest with a few accessories is the only method appropriate in the home workshop. **Photo 9** shows an example.

Explaining in detail how a rest is used is inappropriate here. Briefly, the rest includes a fine feed in two directions: left/right and in/out. With a fixed fence and stops, and with the table capable of being tilted in two directions, this makes it possible to grind quite complex tools accurately.

***

Today, with the advantage of hindsight, the above five items would be amongst the first I would make, should I ever have to set up a completely new workshop again.

Back stop

Another useful item is a back stop (**Photo 10**). This enables you to place parts in the

9. Sharpening engineering tools freehand is not recommended. This grinding rest with simple accessories will produce results almost equal to those achieved by using a tool and cutter grinder.

10. A lathe back stop, particularly useful for repetitive work.

chuck knowing their precise axial position. For example, if you need to make a tubular spacer to a very precise length, fit the back stop and make the part, initially ensuring that it is marginally longer than required. Lock the saddle in place and use the top slide to position the tool for facing the end without moving the saddle or top slide. Remove the part, measure the length, and reposition it against the back stop, feed the top slide as the dimension taken demands, and face end once more. It should now be to the length required. A back stop is even more useful when you need to make a batch of identical parts.

Faceplate-balancing fixture

A more involved item is a faceplate-balancing fixture (**Photo 11**). Balancing an assembly

11./12. (above and above right). This face--balancing fixture enables a faceplate assembly to be accurately balanced so that it will run at the required speed without vibration.

that is fitted to the lathe is always less than satisfactory because of the friction in the lathe's spindle and, in some cases, the problem of

keeping the belts clear of the pulley. Especially when an operation requires a relatively high speed, the lathe can vibrate unacceptably if the assembly is not reasonably balanced. If this cannot be achieved, then it will be necessary to attempt the task at a lower speed, which is not ideal. Using this fixture (**Photo 12**), it is possible to run the lathe at the appropriate speed for the operation in hand, which makes it well worth making!

***

The above should give you some idea of the items that may be useful and, no doubt, you will have other ideas of your own. In this case, do pursue them to a conclusion, as you will not realize their benefit until you have made them. All the above items, and many others, are featured with full manufacturing drawings in the book Model Engineers' Workshop Projects (Workshop Practice Series Number 39).

Chapter 8

Electrics and electronics

Machine controls

The controls provided on modern machines have improved appreciably over recent years, almost certainly because of the demands of industry and educational workshops filtering down to the smaller machines found in the home workshop. Number one requirement is for the system to have a no volt release feature so that the machine cannot start until the start button has been pressed. This means that, if the machine is running when a power failure occurs, it will not automatically restart when the supply is restored.

No volt release

In the home workshop, power sockets often have to be shared between several items. In this case, a machine with just an on/off switch, left in the "on" position, will start when the plug is inserted and the power is switched on.

Note: Where multiple plugs are plugged into a single socket, do ensure that each plug is clearly labelled with details of the device to which it is connected. This is especially important if you switch connected items on/off at the socket switch, although this is not good practice.

1. A no volt switch is worth fitting to machines that are not already provided with this this feature.

Whilst the controls on modern machines will prevent this happening, a machine more than a few years old is unlikely to have a no volt feature. In this case, do **not** rely on the

Foot switch

Another highly desirable feature is a foot switch to stop the machine easily in an emergency. If this is not provided with the machine, the controls should have terminals for connecting one. This facility is particularly important in the case of a drilling machine, where you frequently use one hand to hold the workpiece, either directly or in a vice, and the other to feed the drill; as a result you have no free hand should an emergency occur.

Although a foot switch is less important in the case of the lathe or milling machine, it is a worthwhile addition. This applies especially to the few lathes that have their stop button (and the start button) dangerously placed at the back of the headstock. Should all other features be to your liking and you are considering purchasing such a machine, do ask the supplier to provide the necessary terminals so that you can add a foot switch or a better-placed stop button. Remember, your safety is at stake.

***

Even though faultfinding on this level of equipment is possible without a circuit diagram, having one does make it considerably easier. Therefore, if your machine manual does not include details of the electrics, do request a copy of the service engineer's diagram.

In the workshop

Variable speed drives

These are a relatively modern feature and do have distinct advantages. Even so, the often-quoted advantage of being able to machine at precisely the correct speed is, in my estimation, overstated. However, it avoids having to change belt positions, a chore that often leads to completely the wrong speed being used, even though a better speed is available. Another plus

2. Direct on line starters have a no volt release feature but also provide overload protection and the facility to connect remote controls, typically a foot switch.

switch on the socket, or even an on/off switch on the machine, but purchase and fit a no volt switch (**Photo 1**). A better approach is to fit a direct on line starter (**Photo 2**) because, in addition to the no volt release feature, this has overload protection and better facilities for connecting remove controls, such as a foot switch. However, the overload protection that is included will have a limited current range so you will need to quote the motor's full load current when purchasing the item.

factor is that the control provides a smoother start up and shut down cycle, making it easier on man, motor and machine.

On the down side, the available mechanical power will reduce as the speed reduces, which may be a problem at low speeds. With a belt change system fitted with a 1kW motor, there will still be 1kW of power, even when the lathe is running at its lowest speed. Whilst this will often be more than is required, it will ensure there is adequate torque available for cutting that large diameter thread at minimum speed; some lathes overcome this by providing both an electronic and a mechanical speed control. This may just be in the form of two belt or gear ratios to provide a high and low speed range, thus providing more torque at the lower speeds. Even so, the electronic system will still provide most of the speed control requirements, so changing the belt position will rarely be necessary.

Variable speed drives are available, either already fitted to the machine as purchased or to add to an existing machine. In the former case, you will be in the hands of the machine supplier and you should certainly expect to receive a full service manual for the speed control system because faultfinding on electronic equipment is all but impossible without a diagram.

In the latter case, you may well be purchasing from a specialist drive supplier, who probably also supplies drives in large quantities to industry. The item that you purchase is therefore likely to come from a well-known manufacturer and have a service back-up facility, as demanded by industry. This can be an advantage, especially after many years of use. Even so, you should still expect to receive a service manual.

Fitting a system to an existing machine has the advantage that its mechanical speed-change features will still be available for use should a degree of extra torque be required at the lower speeds.

Digital read-outs

These come in a number of formats, some more useful than others. Digital micrometers are rather more expensive than their mechanical equivalents, but they have the advantage of displaying both metric and imperial dimensions; the additional cost is therefore somewhat offset if you had been intending to purchase micrometers in both units. If not, then as conventional micrometers are relatively easy to read, there seems little to gain from purchasing a digital one.

The situation with digital callipers is quite different because they are similar in price to a vernier calliper and far easier to read. Because of this, they are well worth considering, although you should take note of my later comments regarding reliability (see below). The same comments generally apply to digital height gauges, although these are currently a little more expensive than their mechanical counterparts.

Digital dial gauges have the advantage that there is no need to take note of the number of rotations made by the indicating pointer. Even so, whether this is sufficient to justify the additional expense will depend on how often you will use it for measuring a distance greater than one turn of the dial. Digital dial test indicators are also available but, as their use is more as a comparator, I consider an analogue (mechanical) indicator to be more appropriate. (I remember that the earliest quartz watches all featured digital displays, but these were soon superseded by analogue versions.)

Digital read-outs for machine slides are available but they are only fitted as standard (with a few exceptions) on expensive industrial machines. Devices for adding to existing machines are both available and reasonably priced. However, there is a problem: as there is no standard in terms of machine design, suppliers are unable to provide a read-out that can be fitted immediately. You will therefore need to establish your own method of fitting them.

In general, practically all digital measuring devices are able to display imperial and metric dimensions, which is a definite plus. Another feature is that they can be zeroed at any point, enabling all subsequent dimensions to be taken from a given datum. This can be a disadvantage as well as an advantage: for example, when switching on a digital calliper it is necessary to close the jaws of the device so that it can be zeroed at that point and, if the jaws are dirty, all the following measurements will be inaccurate. The ability to zero the device should therefore be regarded with caution.

CAD/CAM/CNC

The use of computer-aided design (CAD) and computer-aided manufacture (CAM) in the workshop is an attractive prospect. The ability to draw a part on a computer screen and then use the software to control the machine that makes the part is probably the main reason why people with a special interest in this technique introduce this facility into their home workshop.

Very few smaller machines are fully equipped for computer numerical control (CNC) production methods, so any workshop owner wishing to become involved in the process will need to convert a conventional machine. Photos 3 & 4 show a machine that has been fitted with a CNC conversion kit. In this case, the owner is no doubt sufficiently knowledgeable to keep

the system serviced. If not, do take note of my later comments (see Reliability, below).

In my opinion, people who equip their workshop with a CNC machine often do so because installing and using such a machine is a hobby in itself, rather than from any desire to improve productivity(as would be the case in a commercial enterprise). You should therefore think carefully before embarking on such a venture. Note that such a machine cannot

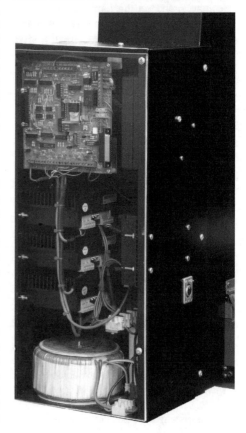

3./4. A CNC conversion kit, (below and right) supplied by Arc Euro Trade and fitted to one of their mill/drills.

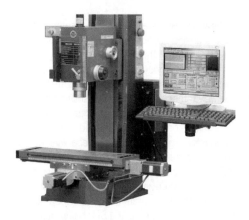

be used manually (i.e. independently of the electronics) and you may still require a purely manual machine. However, if you decide to adopt this approach for its own sake, I am sure it can become an intriguing facet of your hobby.

CAD for drawing only

Producing a drawing for an intended project is far better than designing the item on the job, although for something simple, a hand-drawn sketch or a sketch made using a simple drawing board with a T-square will suffice. However, if you have a computer for other purposes, it is worth installing a CAD program; this should not cost you more than a few tens of pounds, or you may even find a free download that suits your requirements.

This is far too large a subject to cover here, and in any case, as with computers themselves, computer programs develop at an alarming rate. The following is an outline of how CAD can be used to produce a drawing.

1   Draw the final assembly exactly to scale with all the necessary projections. Also show the hidden parts in full, dotted and on each view. (Eventually, you will be able to remove some of this hidden detail to simplify the final drawing.) Do not add any

peripheral data, text, etc. at this stage.

2   Copy the assembly, or a section of it, and choose an individual part. Then delete all the surrounding detail that is not applicable to that part.

3   You will now have an outline of the part. In many cases, some of it, being hidden, will be shown dotted, but it will be to size. The drawing should then be tidied up by eliminating any incorrect detail.

4   You will now have a drawing of the part exactly to scale. You can now dimension this using the program's semi-automatic dimensioning facility. This is considerably simpler than drawing a detail part from scratch and having to refer continually to the assembly drawing for its dimensions.

5   Repeat this process for all the remaining parts.

6   Return to the assembly drawing and remove any hidden detail that you consider unnecessary.

A CAD package also has many other uses. Typically, if you need a dividing plate with 57 divisions, you can use the program to automatically draw 57 very small circles, equally spaced on a given diameter, together with one in the centre of the pitch circle diameter (PCD). This takes no more than a couple of minutes. When printed out, this can be used with a centre punch to mark the positions of the centre hole and the 57 holes and, providing the PCD is not too small, say 100mm, the result should be accurate enough for most applications. You can also use the program to draw a flat plate with a large number of holes at varying distances; this can also be printed out and used in the same manner.

Reliability

Given my background in electronics, readers may be surprised at my note of caution regarding the use of such devices in the home workshop. This is not because of doubts about their benefits but because of their lack of long-term staying power, primarily the potential difficulty in getting them serviced in future years – and here I am talking about 15 years, not 50! The difficulty in maintaining such a system is due partly to its being overtaken by improved and more powerful equipment, and partly to a lack of spares.

On the other hand, the mechanical equipment, such as the lathe and milling machine, will still be usable by your grandchildren – and even your great-grandchildren. This is quite inconceivable in the case of the electronic equipment; even your grandchildren are unlikely to be able to use a machine unless the control system is replaced. So what are my recommendations?

In the case of electronic variable speed drives purchased from a supplier, be sure to acquire a service manual, or at least a circuit diagram. Armed with this, you may just be able to find a local electronic engineer who can fault-find the system. In the early years, the supplier should provide a service but ultimately you will probably have to replace the electronics on block. If you have used an industrial variable speed drive and added the electronics yourself, this will not be a major problem physically, but if the electronics were originally built into the machine's structure, it may not be straightforward. Nevertheless, I believe the advantages outweigh the disadvantages, provided you are prepared to accept them.

I consider digital verniers to be a throwaway item because the cost of servicing them is unlikely to be economic. However, as their electronic content is relatively small, they should have a good lifespan (more components = more likelihood of a failure) but, being relatively new on the market, only time will tell. For me, this does not outweigh their considerable advantages.

Finally, there is the use of CAD/CAM. If you have no real interest in the method for its own sake but only wish to improve your workshop's productivity, I can only refer to an observation by someone with direct knowledge of the situation. He commented that a used manual machine would sell for considerably more than a comparable used CNC machine. Obviously, CNC machines age before their time!

Chapter 9

Machine installation and safety equipment

Machine installation

In most cases, physically, positioning the machine will be straightforward, although it may be hard work. It is only necessary to make sure that its mounting is strong enough for its weight, as even the average mill/drill weighs around 200kg. If the workshop has a wooden floor, the strength of this also needs to be taken into consideration.

Once the machine is in position, even if it is not yet been fastened down, a few initial tasks need to be undertaken. The most obvious is the removal of any surface protection that has been given to the machine. In addition, some minor assembly work may be required.

Next, look for obvious areas that need attention, typically, too much play in the leadscrew, and the table movements being too stiff or too loose. I do not mean to be judgmental, but these are more likely to need attention if you have purchased the machine from the budget end of the market. Even so, budget machines, although they may need a little more attention initially, are still capable of doing good work.

Some machines have adjustments that are

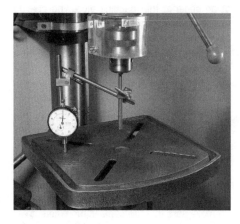

1. Checking a drilling machine table to see whether it has been correctly set.

intended for use while work is in progress, for example, to tilt the drilling machine table or the head of some small milling machines for drilling holes at an angle. Do not assume that these have been set up so that the cutter spindle is perpendicular to the machine's table.

To carry out the required check, mount an indicator as shown in **Photo 1** and rotate the spindle slowly noting the indicator readings.

From these, you will be able to determine the adjustment necessary. Whilst this will enable you to equalize the left/right values, there may still be some error from front to back. In the case of the drilling machine, there may be an adjustment screw that will enable the front of the table to be raised or lowered to correct this error.

For machines other than lathes, which are covered separately (see below), there is little more do other than bolting them into position. However, whilst not essential, it can be helpful to ensure that their worktables are level. This is because, should you wish to set a workpiece at an angle in the machine vice, you can do this using the protractor from a combination set as the protractor mechanism is fitted with a spirit level. Also, before finally bolting a milling machine in place, do traverse the table fully left and right, and back and front, to make certain that there is sufficient room on either side of the machine.

The last task is to connect the machine to the electricity supply. In most cases, this will just be a question of plugging it into the nearest socket. This is perfectly acceptable but, particularly if the socket is some distance from the machine, do make sure that the cable is run where it will not be accidentally damaged; if this cannot be avoided, run it in a piece of surface-mounted trunking.

Lathe installation

Installing a lathe is a much more critical operation, due mainly to the length of the bed and distance between the fixings end to end. However, you should first carry out the general tests described above, especially the adjustment of the slides and saddle movements.

The main problem with the lathe is that, in bolting it to its mounting surface, the bed can be marginally twisted, which will result in the components turned being very slightly tapered. It is true that, if the lathe is only fastened down onto a relatively thin bench top, it will be the bench and not the lathe's bed that will be twisted. However, this overlooks the fact that the bed of the lathe could have twisted since it was machined, due to the continued ageing of the casting, or even the stresses placed on it while being transported from the manufacturer to the user.

If you are surprised by the requirements, bear in mind that the lathe will be expected to turn, say, a 100mm long workpiece parallel and with virtually no measurable difference in diameter from end to end. As a result, it may be necessary to deliberately place a very minute twist in the lathe's bed so that it turns parallel.

In order to meet requirements, the mounting surface must therefore be nominally as strong as the bed itself. If you purchase a lathe complete with stand, you should find that it has a framework below the drip tray to provide this strength. However, you will still need to carry out a series of tests. The following is a very simple explanation of the process, although, if you are new to this, I feel that you should seek other further guidance on the subject.

1. Place a piece of steel about 25mm diameter in the 3-jaw, projecting say 100mm, and reduce it very slightly in diameter over its full length, making a final very shallow cut so that you do not deflect the test piece.

2. Measure both ends and note the result; if the outer end is smaller it will be a case of lifting either the rear fixing at the tailstock end or the front fixing at the headstock end. If it is larger, it will be a case of adjusting the other two fixings. The easiest method

...ectacles and/or a face mask should be ...essential workshop items.

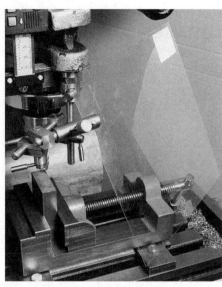

4. It is worth fitting a simple machine guard to protect the operator from swarf and cutting fluid thrown out as a result of the machining operation.

...rotect the operator from items thrown ...by the machine, mainly swarf, but also ...ng oil.

...purpose is, in my estimation, more ...e to the industrial environment, where ...om of mass production can easily lead ...f concentration. Whilst cutting oil is not ...of most home workshops, flying chips ...etal are more common. Of course, this ...happen with all machining operations, ...likely, a simple guard can be rigged up, ...xample shown in **Photo 4**.

...hoes
...n of safety equipment that I cannot ...seeing mentioned in home workshop ...es is a pair of safety shoes. This leads ...ieve that they do not figure prominently ...vorkshops. If this is the case, I think it

is a dangerous oversight and I would strongly recommend that you obtain a pair and wear them. A dropped chuck or vice may cause considerable discomfort but more importantly, could do permanent damage. There is really no excuse for working without a pair because they are not that much more expensive than normal shoes.

Ear defenders
Noise in the small metalworking workshop is not that great a problem, so hearing protection is perhaps not essential. However, I have noticed that some machining operations on the lathe can produce a quite unpleasant sound and, even if it is not dangerous, it is worth escaping from it. A pair of ear defenders costs no more than a few pounds so there is no reason why they should not be part of the workshop's safety equipment.

2. *Jacking screw under a lathe's foot, used on installation for setting the lathe to turn parallel.*

of making these very small adjustments is to use a jacking screw at each fixing (see Photo 2). Otherwise, it will be a case of adding shims, which can be a very tedious trial-and-error operation. Even so, it is an essential requirement before putting your lathe to work.

3. The next stage is to turn a test piece between centres, say 150mm long by 25mm diameter and turn this over its length. Again, measure the diameter at both ends and, using the tailstock's set over adjustment, make adjustments until a parallel test piece results. This test must be carried out after the one above.

Bearing these requirements in mind, it is interesting that one much respected lathe manufacturer grinds the top surface of the lathe's bed so that it is very slightly raised in the middle. The reason for this is to compensate for the drop in the bed that results when the weight of the saddle is added on assembly, and for the downward pressure that results when a cut is being taken.

Some smaller lathes will not have the facility

to make the above
will probably have to
received.

Safety equipment
I consider the subject
be mostly a matter of
not intend to go into it
I know from experienc
take precautions, so a
of place.

Firstly, a first aid kit in
because, even with the
will happen, hopefully r
to equip the workshop
barrier cream and an af
use the barrier cream a
it much easier to clean
a work session.

The next thing to consid
There is a wide range
intended to protect th
aspect of the task being

Face protection
In terms of face protec
comes to mind is sa
come in a wide range
thick frames and quit
I find limit the field of
would suggest, are tho
wraparound lens, as sh
has the added advanta
worn over prescription
a greater degree of pro
is a face mask (also sho

Machine guards
Machine guards serve t

1. to prevent the ope
contact with the m

3. *Safety
consider*

2. to
on
c

The fir
applica
the bo
to a los
a featu
of hot
does n
but if it
like the

Safety
One it
recolle
magaz
me to b
in such

Chapter 10

The lathe

Unless your workshop activity can be undertaken with hand tools only, perhaps with a drilling machine, then the lathe is the one essential machine tool. In fact, for many years, the lathe was the only machine available in the majority of home workshops; it was used not only for turning operations but also for drilling and milling. Whilst lathe-only set-ups are now in the minority, there are still many workshop owners who produce very interesting items using this format. Therefore, if you feel restricted to having such a workshop, do not be put off by its limitations. Whilst these may limit the physical size of a project, in terms of complexity and satisfaction gained it can be the equal of a more highly equipped workshop.

Lathe-only user

If you expect to fall into this category permanently, or at least for a good number of years, then the choice of lathe is more important than if you are intending to add other machines to your collection. However, I would suggest that, whatever your limitations, be they finance or space, you consider including a small bench drilling machine.

Drilling using a lathe, although possible, is not

1. It is possible, but not ideal, to use a lathe as an alternative to a drilling.

a very straightforward operation, as shown in **Photo 1**. In this photograph, the tailstock has been fitted with a faceplate, using an adapter, and the workpiece is fed using the tailstock's feed. This method has its limitations and a small drilling machine will make drilling operations very much easier.

Milling operations are a more practical proposition but a standard lathe has some limitations that will have to be overcome. With the cutter in the lathe's mandrel and the workpiece mounted on the cross slide, the

2. Simple milling can be carried out on a standard lathe but the lack of the third axis limits considerably what can be achieved.

3. A vertical slide provides the third axis for milling.

saddle will control the depth of cut and the cross slide will feed the workpiece to make the cut. However, there is no provision for adjusting the workpiece relative to the cutter in the third axis.

In a few cases, this can be overcome by careful placing of the workpiece, as shown in **Photo 2**, where an enclosed slot is being milled. In this case, the angle plate was first held in the vice with the working face horizontal, making it relatively easy to position the workpiece so that the slot would eventually be machined correctly. Of course, you do need to know the exact height of the lathe's mandrel above the top surface of the cross slide. Once you have measured this, you should make a note of the measurement and keep it on record. (It is a good idea to keep a notebook in the workshop for such records.)

For more complex operations, the only option is to purchase a vertical slide (**Photo 3**). The operation being carried out here is the same as that shown in **Photo 2**, but this time aided by the vertical slide. As a result, positioning the slot is much easier and potentially more accurate.

Therefore, we already have two essential items: a T-slotted cross slide and a vertical slide. Whilst not quite in the essential category, the size of

the lathe is another important consideration. In terms of turning requirements, one of the smaller lathes may easily cater for your intended interest but be totally inadequate for the milling tasks that you are likely to attempt. This is because, whilst a workpiece maybe small, the additional items (vice, angle plate, clamps, supports, etc.) can make the assembly quite large. The cross and vertical slides must therefore be large enough to accommodate them. Because of this therefore, you should choose a lathe with substantial cross and vertical slides, which will probably require a lathe with a minimum centre height of around 90mm. (See also comments below on lathes with a built-in milling head.).

A chuck suitable for holding milling cutters will also be required because it is not acceptable to hold cutters in a drill chuck, or even a 3-jaw chuck. The question of suitable chucks is covered in Chapter 14 on milling machine accessories.

The lathe (with milling machine)

Where a milling machine is included in the workshop, the lathe's main purpose will be to produce all the turned items. However, even if the machine will be used for only a limited range of tasks, the choice is by no means easy. This is because the range of lathes available, considering price, features and size, is far greater than that of any other machine likely to find its way into the home workshop.

4. A 90mm centre height lathe (Warco).

Size

Once you have set your budget, at least provisionally, you first choice will be the size of lathe. This will typically be between the Warco, with a centre height of 90mm and a between-centres distance of 300mm (**Photo 4**), and the larger Wabeco from Pro Machine Tools Ltd (**Photo 5**), with a centre height of 135mm and a between-centres distance of 600mm. Between the two, size-wise, is the very popular Series Seven Lathe produced by Myford (**Photo 6**) This has a centre height of 88mm and a between-centres distance of 480mm. There are also smaller and larger lathes that may suit those with particular needs.

5. A 135mm centre height lathe (Wabeco).

Bearing in mind its intended use, you can make your choice. However, as a very rough rule of thumb, I would suggest a centre height of at least twice the maximum anticipated bar diameter to be turned. This will give some leeway on the rare occasion when you need to turn larger diameters. Even so, do take account of the fact that the between-centres diameter is limited by the height of the cross slide above the bed's surface. Another vital consideration is that too large is almost as bad as too small, particularly if your intended projects require a lot of very small-diameter work, in which case, clock-making for example, it is better to err on the small side. It is a little more difficult to advise on the between-centres length other than to say do consider this carefully. For example, an

6. The popular Myford Series Seven, with a centre height of 88mm.

unnecessarily long lathe may take up space that could be better used for other things.

Speed range

The range of speeds is a vital consideration.

For a lot of small-diameter work, say less than 8mm, a relatively high speed should be considered essential. For this, I would suggest a minimum of 2500 rpm, preferably higher. For very occasional work at these diameters, a lower speed may suffice, but I would suggest a minimum top speed of 1500 rpm whatever the lathe's purpose. At the other end of the speed range, two operations will call for very low speeds: cutting screw threads and turning large and irregularly shaped items, probably on the faceplate.

For screw cutting, you should aim for a maximum speed of 50 rpm, although the novice may find even this to be on the fast side, especially for short threads that do not allow much thinking time. As an example, when cutting an 8 TPI thread 1/2in. long at a speed of 100 rpm, there are just 2.4 seconds between the start and end of the thread. The situation is even more difficult if the thread being cut is an internal one where visibility is restricted.

For screw cutting, therefore, it is solely a case of the operator's speed of reaction rather than the machine's ability to cut the thread. As many lathes do not have a low enough speed for screw cutting, it is common practice to fit a handle to the lathe's mandrel so that the lathe can be turned manually. To my knowledge, these are not supplied by manufacturers so it will be a case of making your own.

For tasks other than screw cutting, a minimum of 200 rpm is a good speed to aim for, unless you anticipate machining large and irregularly shaped items on the faceplate on a regular basis. For this, I would suggest 100 rpm maximum as the lowest speed.

For many years, good work has been carried out on lathes with a limited number of fixed speeds, sometimes as few as three, but more often six. A greater number, although desirable, cannot therefore be considered absolutely essential. Obviously, the wider the speed range the larger the number of fixed speeds required; as a guide, I suggest twelve for 50–2500 rpm and six for 500–1500 rpm.

Speed control in the past has invariably been by means of belts and stepped pulleys, with a gear chain to provide the lowest speeds. The gear chain was usually known as the back gear, probably because it was mounted at the back of the lathe's mandrel (although I could be wrong), but larger lathes, in particular those for industry, were equipped with fully geared heads. However, the move towards electronic variable speed drives is becoming much more apparent.

The ability to set precise speeds can be an advantage, although I think this is rather over-rated providing the lathe has a good number of fixed speeds. The real advantage is the immediate availability of any speed without the need to change belt positions. This can be a chore at the best of times and a deterrent from using the best speed available. In addition, the lathe starts up, runs and slows down more smoothly. Another less obvious advantage is that, when facing, or parting off a large diameter, the speed can be increased as the diameter reduces.

However, on the down side, reliability and the question of the availability of spares over a long time period needs looking at very carefully (see Chapter 8).

Drive clutch

Electric motors require a very high starting current and, if single phase, a centrifugal switch to switch out the starting capacitor during starting. As a result, the starting sequence is an arduous operation, particularly where an operation, such as screw cutting, involves

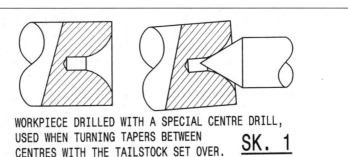

WORKPIECE DRILLED WITH A SPECIAL CENTRE DRILL, USED WHEN TURNING TAPERS BETWEEN CENTRES WITH THE TAILSTOCK SET OVER. **SK. 1**

frequent starting and stopping. To reduce the demand on the motor, some lathes have a mechanical clutch to start and stop the machine. Whilst by no means an essential feature, this is highly desirable for motors switched with a direct on line (DOL) starter or a simple switch. As DOL starters are readily available, manual switches should no longer be considered an acceptable method of controlling a motor.

Top slide

Another feature of lathe design is the provision of a top slide, which is mounted on the cross slide and carries the cutting tool. This is sometimes referred to as a compound slide. Its main feature is that it can be rotated, allowing surfaces to be machined at an angle. On some lathes, it will rotate a full 360° whilst, on others, it will have a limited range. The limited range provided should be adequate for the majority of the tasks, although a greater angle may occasionally be useful.

As the slide is normally set parallel with the saddle, it is in no way essential for most of the tasks undertaken. Because of this, some lathes, mostly smaller ones, do not have a top slide. If you are considering purchasing one of these, you should therefore ask yourself if the lack of an easy way to machine tapers is acceptable, although many of these lathes do have a top slide available as an optional extra.

The disadvantage of the top slide when turning tapers is that its limited movement makes it difficult to produce longer tapers. In this case, the taper may have to be machined in two sections and, although far from impossible, this is not ideal. Most workshop owners, including me, will use this method to get by.

However, there are two other methods of turning tapers that may be provided with the lathe. The first, which is available on most lathes of medium size and larger, is the ability to set the tailstock off centre. This enables workpieces mounted between centres to be turned with a taper. However, beyond a certain angle, the misalignment of the centres makes the method inappropriate. Using a special centre drill that produces a curved centre (see Sk. 1) enables the angle to be increased a little but, even so, the taper is limited to just a few degrees.

The other method, and by far the most adaptable, relies on a device that is mounted behind the bed and coupled to the cross slide to provide the taper. Unfortunately, whilst very good, it is not available with most lathes, and where it is available, it is an extra rather than being supplied as standard. Very briefly, the cross slide is disconnected from its feed screw and moved in or out by the taper attachment as the saddle is traversed along the bed.

Neither of these two taper-turning methods is likely to be of use to the majority of workshop owners and their absence should not affect the choice of lathe. They do, however, have the advantage that the lathe's auto fine feed can be used, thus enabling a better finish to be easily achieved than when using the top slide.

Screw cutting

For screw cutting to be carried out on a centre lathe, a series of gears connects the lathe's mandrel to the leadscrew, which then moves the lathe's saddle. In simple terms, assume that the leadscrew has a pitch of 2mm and the gear chain a ratio of 1:1. In this case, both the mandrel and leadscrew will run at the same speed. Therefore, the thread cut will be the equal of the leadscrew, namely 2mm. However, if the ratio is 2:1 and the leadscrew runs at half the speed of the mandrel, the pitch will be 1mm. By careful choice of gears, a very wide range of pitches can be cut.

The gear chain, however, needs to be set up manually. In some cases, it will comprise three drivers/three driven and, in other cases, two drivers/two driven. As the direction of rotation of the leadscrew will change depending on whether two or three sets of gears are being employed, this could result in some threads being right-handed and some left-handed. To overcome this, a series of small gears operates between the gear on the lathe's mandrel and the first driver. These are on a lever that engages either a single gear or two gears in series, and enables the rotation to be changed as the gear chain requires. This assembly is called a "tumbler reverse" Another important advantage of the tumbler reverse is that it can be set to a mid-position that disconnects the gear on the lathe's mandrel from the first driver, avoiding the gear chain having to run when not required.

The changewheel on some lathes is always configured as two drivers/two driven, in which

7. A gearbox makes setting up for screw cutting a simple and rapid operation.

case there is no need for a tumbler reverse and one is not fitted. However, this means that left-handed threads cannot be cut easily. In most cases, however, a small idler can be included in the chain to overcome this problem. I should add that a few very small lathes do not have a facility for screw cutting.

Changing the gears to enable a thread to be cut is not only time-consuming but also loses the fine feed that is set up using the same gear system. This makes it a deterrent from cutting threads, although some lathes overcome this by having a gearbox fitted for the purpose (**Photo 7**). This gearbox enables the lathe to be set up for both threads and fine feeds in a matter of seconds and, if cutting threads is a frequent requirement, then a lathe with this facility is definitely worth considering. However, it will limit your choice because, to my knowledge, no small-size lathe (i.e. with a centre height of less than 70mm) is fitted with this facility.

Saddle half nut

The saddle half nut is another item that is not fitted on all lathes. Being split, it can be opened in order to disengage the nut from the leadscrew, permitting the saddle to be moved rapidly along the lathe's bed. The quick traverse is achieved using a rack and pinion, with the pinion being rotated using a hand wheel on the saddle. Lathes without this feature require the leadscrew to be manually turned to move the saddle. For example, a lathe with a 2mm pitch leadscrew will require 50 turns to move the saddle only 100mm. If you have already used a lathe fitted with a half nut, you may find having to make so many turns of the leadscrew unacceptable. However, if it is your first lathe, you will probably accept it as the norm, but you should give this some thought.

A common misconception is that the purpose of the half nut is for cutting screw threads, whereas its true purpose is to enable the saddle to be moved rapidly along the lathe's bed. It is, however, true that, when cutting threads, the position in which the nut is closed is vital to ensure that subsequent cuts line up with those already taken. This appears to give the half nut a measure of importance for the task. However, lathes that do not have a half nut are still capable of cutting threads, and there is no possibility of crossed threads, just the need to reverse the lathe back to the starting position. In this case, a lathe fitted with a reversing motor will be a definite plus; otherwise, the lathe will need to be run back manually.

Thread dial indicator

Where a half nut is fitted and used during threading tasks, a thread dial indicator (**Photo 8**) is essential. This is used to indicate when to close the half nut for each subsequent cut. If the thread being cut is a multiple of the leadscrew pitch, it can be closed randomly. For other cuts (odd, even or half pitches), the half nut can only be closed in certain positions. For more complex numbers, such as metric pitches on an imperial lathe, the half nut must remain closed. In this case, it will be necessary to reverse the cutting tool back to the start.

8. A thread dial indicator is required to ensure the half nut is closed in the correct position when screw cutting.

Powered cross slide feed

On a small number of lathes, the cross slide can be power fed. Personally, I find this of limited use with normal turning. However, it is very useful when milling on the lathe using the vertical slide. The need to make multiple passes in order to surface an area makes the facility all but essential for me, especially as the relative lack of rigidity of the set-up requires many lightweight cuts to be taken, many more than when working with a milling machine.

Milling head

Milling on the lathe has already been discussed (see above) in terms of using the lathe's mandrel to hold the cutter and by adding a vertical slide to provide the third axis. Milling heads with a vertical down feed are available for fitting to the lathe to provide the third axis. In this case, the

9. Rear-mounted milling head fitted to a Wabeco lathe.

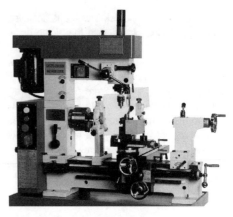

10. A milling head permanently mounted on the lathe's headstock (Chester).

saddle and cross feed provide two of the axes and the head provides the third axis, rather like the typical mill/drill but with a much smaller capacity.

For many years, these milling heads have been provided as an optional extra for adding to the lathe, either fixed to the outer end of the bed or mounted behind it on a bracket (**Photo 9**), the latter being the most common. More recently, the milling head has been supplied as part of the lathe, mounted above the headstock (**Photo 10**). Compared with using a vertical slide, both methods have the advantage of a horizontal work table, making it easier to position the workpiece for machining. However, I do feel that they may not live up to expectation in terms of robustness and the resulting speed of metal removal.

Another factor is the cutter to work table distance, which appears to be far too great on the modern versions. Some manufacturers appear to agree with this and provide a rising device in the form of a channel to lift the workpiece nearer the cutter. This has two potential problems: the rising device has a smaller area for mounting the workpiece and, with it now being well above the slide's dovetails, I am concerned that this may affect rigidity. Even so, if you are limited to a single machine and are prepared to accept that a lack of robustness may affect its ability to remove metal quickly, then these machines have a lot in their favour. Personally, I would like to see the machine under power and working before making a purchase.

Chapter 11

The lathe accessories

Once you have decided which lathe to purchase, you will still need a large number of accessories if it is to function adequately. In many cases, some of these will be supplied as standard with the lathe. This may seem like an advantage, and it is in many cases, but it prevents you having a choice over the size and quality of some items, for example, a 3-jaw chuck.

Cutters
This is a vast subject so I can only comment on the types available and list their advantages and disadvantages. Readers should consult other publications for more in-depth information.

Replaceable tip cutters
Typical versions of replaceable tip tools, sometimes referred to as indexable tools, are shown in **Photo 1**. With a few exceptions, such as parting tools (shown left and right), the tips come in three main shapes, round, three-sided and four-sided, permitting the tip to be rotated to a new edge when that being used becomes blunt.

This is very much an oversimplification

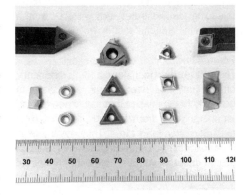

1. Lathe tools with replaceable tips.

because they are available to a wide range of specifications, with changes to material, finish, shape, size, sharpness and radius on the corners all making up a variable item. However, the limited range stocked by most suppliers is general purpose and sufficient for home workshop tasks.

Also shown in the photograph (rear centre) are triangular tips with a screw thread form on

87

each corner for use when thread cutting. These are available in two forms: one with just the appropriate angle and a small tip radius (root of the thread cut), and the other with a shape that also produces the radius on the crest of the thread. The advantage of the first is that it can be used for any pitch for a particular thread form, say metric, but without producing the radius on the crest. The second, however, can only be used for a single pitch, although it does produce a full form thread and is therefore the better choice.

A disadvantage of tipped tools is the difficulty of making them in small sizes for internal work, either plain bores or threaded. Even so, smaller sizes are becoming available, as the smaller threading tool illustrates; this will start from a minimum hole diameter of 8mm.

Permanently tipped cutters

These have a tip of tungsten carbide permanently brazed onto a steel shank and conform generally to the shapes that have been ground for many years from HSS blanks. A typical range is shown in **Photo 2**. Their advantage is their ability to cope with difficult materials (such as iron castings, with their inherent problem of hard surface spots) and rigidity (assuming you purchase them in a large shank size and mount

them directly onto the lathe's top slide). They can also be sharpened, although the need for a special wheel to carry out this task detracts slightly from this advantage. Moreover, they are very much cheaper than a replaceable tip with suitable holder.

High-speed steel (HSS) cutters

For many years, HSS cutters have been the main type of lathe tool; prior to this, similar tools made from a carbon-content steel were used. **Photo 3** shows a range of HSS cutters, including a very small boring tool (left) and a tool for cutting a worm wheel (right). Both are typical of tools that are not available commercially with other systems.

Unfortunately, their advantages are generally outweighed by their disadvantages. However, one advantage, the ability to be ground into almost any shape, makes them indispensable, because some requirements cannot be met by other methods. Another major advantage is that it is possible to hone them to a very sharp edge, making extremely fine cuts possible, as necessary when working to very precise dimensions.

3. High-speed steel lathe tools: small boring tool (left), worm wheel cutter (right). HSS tools are essential for special shapes that cannot be obtained with the other two types of cutter.

2. Lathe tools with permanent (brazed) tips.

4. *Mounting the lathe tool directly onto the top slide is not ideal but may sometimes be necessary.*

On the down side, the initial shaping of the cutter from a blank is a time-consuming task and not that simple. In addition, the edge produced is not as long lasting as with other types of cutter, and it is particularly prone to damage if used to machine the outer skin from a casting.

Which type?

As a guide, I would advise you to use replaceable tip tools for all your basic turning, namely outside diameter and end face work. For most people, this will be 90% plus of the tasks undertaken. Brazed tipped tools can then be reserved for the initial machining of castings, leaving HSS tools for specialised applications.

Another decision to be made is the size of shank, but this will depend on your choice of tool holder. Regarding this, do take note though of my comment above regarding permanent tip tools and their mounting directly onto the lathe's top slide

Tool holders

Before purchasing any cutting tools, you will need to decide on the method of holding them, as this will often affect the sizes of shank that can be used. There are a number of methods, the simplest being a clamp that holds the tool directly onto the top slide's mounting surface, as illustrated in **Photo 4**. Although simple, this method is not really practical for day-to-day use because of the need for packing to bring each tool up to the required height. It should therefore be used only when circumstances dictate, for example, when using a cutter with a much larger shank than normal.

Next in terms of simplicity is the four-way tool post (**Photo 5**). This tends to get a bad press due to the need for packing to bring the tool up to centre height. In the past, my approach has been to ensure that I have a wide range of shim thicknesses ready cut to size, marked with their thickness and stored for easy use.

5. *A four-way post makes the four most used tools almost instantaneously available.*

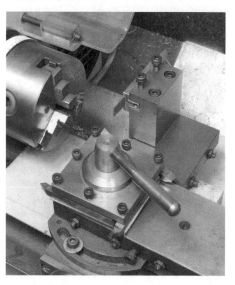

6. Setting the height of the lathe tool is quickly done with a calibrated tool height gauge.

7. Quick-change tool holders are not as rapid as a four-way post but more convenient if you wish to have more than four tools readily available.

Choosing the required packing thickness is not difficult, especially if you use a calibrated tool height gauge (**Photo 6**). With your four most-used tools set up, changing from tool to tool is almost instantaneous, and much quicker even than using a quick-change system. If you have already chosen the system, it might be worth considering a second post to give you a choice of eight tools. This is not expensive as it is quite easy to make your own tool posts.

Should you see a need for a wide range of quickly available tools, a quick-change system would be the method to choose. However, this can be very expensive if you need more than a few holders. In this case, you may like to consider making your own, as shown in **Photo 7**. These are relatively easy to make because the system avoids the need for machining dovetails.

When using a quick-change tool system, whether commercial or shop made, the tool overhangs the end of the top slide (**Photo 8**). As a result, this system is marginally less robust than a four-way tool post. This will not normally be a problem, but it may be a consideration if you have a relatively lightweight lathe.

8. When using a quick-change tool holder system, the tool overhangs the end of the top slide and may cause rigidity problems on a light-duty lathe or if a very heavy cut is attempted.

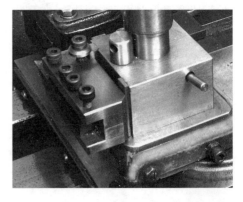

9. A rear tool post is all but essential for parting off

Whatever tool-holding method you decide to use on the top slide, there is one tool that will not work at its best in this position: the parting off tool. Although some quick-change systems include holders for these, they are not to be recommended, unless your lathe is a very heavy-duty industrial machine. Without going into the mechanics, this is because parting off with a tool mounted on a rear tool post is all but essential on the average home workshop lathe. This can be with a post that takes a single parting off tool, or a post with a turret that permits two tools to be fitted (**Photo 9**).

Unfortunately, even though many people, apart from me, consider a rear-mounted tool post to be essential, they do not seem to be available for many lathes, either as standard or as an optional accessory. Fortunately, it is not difficult to make and fit it yourself, although you may need to drill and tap the cross slide to fix the post (as was the case for the post shown in Photo 5).

Other tool holders have been used in the past, which you may come into contact with, especially if you are purchasing a second hand machine, but the above are now almost entirely the standard.

Work holders
There is a lot of equipment for work holding on the lathe, but many are specialised and designed for a specific task, for example, the stub mandrel. Commonly available work-holding methods amount to just four: a faceplate, jawed chucks, collet chucks and between centres.

Faceplates
As faceplates are not the easiest method to use, they are reserved for situations where the workpiece cannot be held in a jawed chuck, typically a large casting or an irregularly shaped item. The security of the workpiece and its clamping components is of paramount importance; if at all possible, any holes in the workpiece should be used for the screws that clamp it to the faceplate. This is the ideal method but, unfortunately, it is frequently not possible. In this case, the method normally adopted is that used on the milling machine: a clamp bar with packing under one end and the item being machined under the other. Whilst this is acceptable on the machine table, it poses a potential problem on the faceplate, namely, should a clamp become loose, the packing piece can be thrown from the assembly as it rotates at speed.

This problem can be overcome by using the system illustrated in **Sk. 1**, in which the packing is tapped and first clamped to the faceplate prior to the nut being used to clamp the item being machined. Unfortunately, as far as I know, this system, also shown in **Photo 10**, is not available commercially.

After mounting your workpiece on the faceplate, you will probably find that the assembly is unbalanced, resulting in severe vibration when the machine is run up to speed. To achieve a balance, suitably placed weights, typically the square plate (bottom right) must be added to

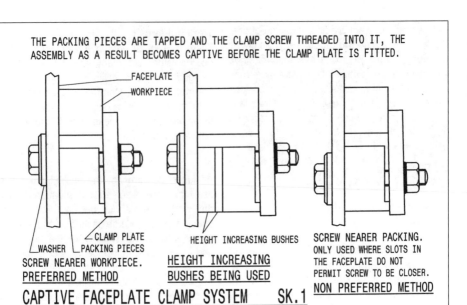

THE PACKING PIECES ARE TAPPED AND THE CLAMP SCREW THREADED INTO IT, THE
ASSEMBLY AS A RESULT BECOMES CAPTIVE BEFORE THE CLAMP PLATE IS FITTED.

FACEPLATE
WORKPIECE

CLAMP PLATE
WASHER PACKING PIECES
SCREW NEARER WORKPIECE.
PREFERRED METHOD

HEIGHT INCREASING BUSHES
HEIGHT INCREASING
BUSHES BEING USED

SCREW NEARER PACKING.
ONLY USED WHERE SLOTS IN
THE FACEPLATE DO NOT
PERMIT SCREW TO BE CLOSER.
NON PREFERRED METHOD

CAPTIVE FACEPLATE CLAMP SYSTEM   SK.1

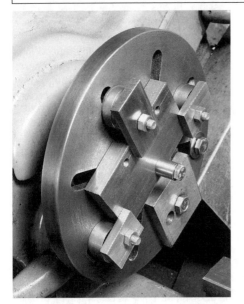

10. This workpiece clamping system has the advantage of being captive, ensuring that it will not be thrown should it become loose while in use.

the assembly. Whilst this can be done on the lathe, the spindle's mass (including its pulleys) and relatively high friction means that a near-balance is not that easy to achieve. A free-running faceplate fixture will be of considerable help but, again, these fixtures are not available commercially and will have to be made in the workshop (see Chapter 7).

Jawed chucks

These chucks commonly come with either 3 or 4 jaws, although 2- and 6-jaw chucks are available. To my knowledge, 3-jaw chucks are always self-centring (i.e. the jaws move together), whilst, in the case of the 4-jaw, the jaws are mostly moved individually, although 4-jaw self-centring chucks are available.

The novice should dissuaded from the opinion that the 3-jaw is for round and hexagonal items while the 4-jaw is just for square or rectangular workpieces. The most important factor to understand is that, whilst the 3-jaw chuck is self-centring, it is not precise. Because of this, the workpiece may run off centre, typically by 0.05mm (0.1mm TIR, total indicator reading), sometimes more. Whilst this may be more than adequate for most tasks, there are occasions when this is not the case. This is particularly so where a part has to be removed from and replaced into the chuck, because the part is unlikely to be returned to exactly the same place.

Therefore, where concentricity is important, the only option is to use the 4-jaw chuck, because this enables each jaw to be positioned independently, thus enabling precise centring to be achieved. Consequently, if you cannot afford to purchase both types of chuck, you should settle for just a 4-jaw. This may not be so convenient for many jobs, but it will satisfy more requirements than a 3-jaw

11. One of the two common methods of fixing items to the lathe's mandrel is by means of a screw.

Incidentally, precision 3-jaw chucks are available but they still have some error and, as a result, are not adequate for the most demanding applications.

The jaws
Self-centring chucks are supplied with two sets of jaws: one with a vertical face for clamping bar material and the other with a stepped form for holding items such as disks. They also allow larger diameters to be held but, because of the limited depth of grip provided by the stepped jaws, they may not be suitable for use with overly long parts. The jaws of independent chucks have a single set of jaws, but these can be reversed to provide the same facility.

Self-centring chucks can also be fitted with soft jaws that can be machined to match the requirements of the part to be machined, typically shallow steps to hold a thin disk-shaped workpiece. These jaws are rarely supplied as standard with the chuck and will

have to be purchased separately. Although not frequently used, they are all but essential for the occasional task and should be considered an essential workshop item.

Backplates
Unfortunately, there has been no standard in the past with respect to the lathe's mandrel nose, and whilst there are only two common methods, screwed (**Photo 11**) and flanged (**Photo 12**), there is considerable variation in terms of dimensions. It is therefore impracticable for chuck manufacturers to produce chucks that will mount directly onto the lathe, except for a few very common forms, such as the Myford screwed nose and some industrial standards.

To overcome this, an adapter, usually known as a backplate, must be fitted to the rear of the chuck. If you have purchased a new lathe, the supplier will have chucks already fitted with a backplate and obtaining a suitable chuck will

12. The other common method of fixing items to the lathe's mandrel is by means of a flange.

13. The most common forms of collet currently available: Morse (front), R8 (centre), ER (left and right), 5C (left and right of centre). The R8 collet is only used on the milling machine.

be a straightforward process. However, if you are purchasing a secondhand lathe, or a special chuck for your new lathe, you will have to carry out some machining to enable the chuck to fit.

If your lathe is relatively recent, or a very well known make, a backplate should be available already machined for fitting to the lathe. In this case, the only requirement is to machine the outer face to fit the register in the rear of the chuck to be fitted. Holes will also have to be drilled for fitting the backplate to the rear of the chuck.

If your lathe is of a relatively rare make, it will be necessary to purchase a backplate casting and machine it for fitting both to the lathe and to the chuck itself.

Collet chucks

As demonstrated by the examples of collets shown in Photo 13, there can be substantial differences. Collets are not used solely on the lathe but, being dual purpose, are also used for both work holding and tool holding. They are therefore equally at home on the milling machine and the lathe. Although I discuss collets in detail here, I have added further

comments, as appropriate, in Chapter 14 on milling machine accessories .

Although they do have major differences, collets all have one thing in common: accuracy! This makes them particularly useful for clock-making, where concentricity is vital because of the many spindles that these mechanisms require. Concentricity is similarly desirable when holding milling cutters, etc. On the down side, for most types, an individual collet can only grip over a very small range: typically +0.0–0.1mm, or perhaps +0.0– 0.2mm for the larger sizes. Therefore, the part being held must have a diameter within the collet's very limited range.

The types of collet can be grouped in a number of ways, for example, those that are mounted directly into a machine's taper as opposed to those that require a dedicated holder. In this respect, only two types are commonly available: Morse and R8 tapers (see photograph).

The advantage of these collets is that, being within the machine's spindle, there is no overhang, which results in greater rigidity. In addition, the increased maximum distance between cutter and machine table may be helpful in a few cases. The collet is closed by being drawn into the taper using a draw bar through the machine's spindle, but here the similarity ends. As the Morse taper has a very small internal angle, the collet will stick in the machine spindle and will need to be loosened with a gentle tap on the end of the draw bar. The R8 taper, however, with its much larger angle, is self-releasing. Because they need to be used with a draw bar, lengths of material cannot pass through them and, therefore, in most cases, they are only useful for holding cutters.

As far as I know, the R8 taper is found only on milling machines, where it is becoming popular, perhaps because of its use on the very popular Bridgeport mills.

In reference to the need for a draw bar, Myford, and possibly other companies, supply Morse taper collets that are pushed into the taper using a closing ring screwed onto the lathe's mandrel nose. These have a groove into which the closing ring engages so that the ring can jack out the collet to loosen the part being held. This is rather like the ER type collets discussed below. The important advantage is that they can be used to hold a bar that can pass through them.

Another way of grouping collet systems is by their working angles: nominally 2° in the case of Morse taper collets and up to 10° for the 5C type (see photograph). Obviously, for a given closing force, the wider the angle the looser is the grip. Because of this, only the shallower angles are suitable for holding milling cutters. These include Morse, R8 and ER series; 5C collets at 10° are largely used for work holding.

The final grouping is by their gripping range. Here, the ER series (see photograph) stands out from the others, being able individually to grip diameters over a range of 1mm. For others,

the range will be no more than 0.2mm and so an individual collet will be required for each diameter to be held, both imperial and metric. On the other hand, ER collets are made in 1mm increments, which means that any diameter, imperial of metric, within the series size range can be held.

Gripping range
Morse collets are commonly made in three sizes, Morse 1, 2 and 3, and they hold up to 8, 12 and 18mm respectively. R8 is a single-size collet system with collets up to 20mm. ER collets are available in seven series: ER11, 16, 20, 25, 32, 40 and 50. Maximum sizes gripped range from 7mm for the smallest size up to 34mm for the largest.

5C collets are again a single single-size system but with some distinct advantages, such as a much wider range of collets and collet fixtures. They are the only ones where shapes other than round are freely available, as are fixtures for using them on the milling machine. Their capacity is 28mm diameter, with 18mm being the maximum for both square and hexagonal collets.

For all collets, I have quoted gripping sizes in metric terms but, generally speaking, comparable ranges are available in imperial dimensions.

Closing method
One other comparison worthy of mention is the method used to tighten the collets onto the item being held. As mentioned above, Morse and R8 collets are pulled into the taper, but ER collets are pushed into the holder by means of a closing ring. However, at 8°, the collet may occasionally be prone to stick and so, to prevent this happening, the collet has a groove into which the closing ring engages, allowing it

to jack out the collet when it is being opened.

5C collets are the most variable because they can be either pulled or pushed into the internal taper. The small end of the collet has both external and internal threads that enable draw systems to be attached that pull the collet into its mating taper. However, some fixtures have a closing ring that pushes the collet into its mating taper.

Dead length systems
In most collet systems, the degree by which the collet enters the internal taper depends on the diameter of the workpiece. When carrying out a second operation on batches of components that have a permitted tolerance on diameter, this change of position can be a problem if the component has a shoulder that needs to register on the front face of the collet.

To overcome this, systems are available in which the collet is held in a fixed position and the internal taper moves forward to close the collet. These are very specialised and are only available from a limited number of sources. They are, of course, only applicable for batch production work and are unlikely to be of use in the home workshop. A little more is said on this subject in the discussion of milling machines (Chapter 14), although systems that exhibit this feature are available for use on some lathes.

Collet holders
As mentioned above, the use of the R8 collet is limited to the milling machine. As Morse taper collets mount directly into the machine's taper, no additional components are needed other than a draw bar.

One method of using the ER series collets, at least the smaller sizes, is to use a holder with a Morse taper (**Photo 14**), although this makes it suitable only for holding cutters. As a result, it

14. This form of collet holder is only suitable for holding cutters as it cannot accept bar material.

will only be of use to the workshop owner who carries out milling operations on the lathe.

Photo 15 shows a holder for ER32 collets that is screwed onto the mandrel's threaded nose and allows it to be used for bar material. Flange-mounted versions are also available for both the ER series and the 5C collet system. In

15. Being screwed onto the lathe's mandrel nose, this collet holder enables bar material to pass completely through and is therefore more suitable for use on the lathe.

most cases, these need a backplate, like the jawed chucks (see above), to enable them to be fitted onto the lathe.

Worthwhile?
I cannot suggest to the new workshop owner that collets for work-holding on the lathe are in any way essential, except, as already mentioned, for clock-making. As working at small diameters requires relatively high speeds and running a collet chuck is a much safer and more pleasant operation than running a large-jawed chuck. In these circumstances, they are worth considering

"Must haves"
In addition to the above items, not all of which are absolutely essential, there are a few other items that do fit into the essential category. The following are mentioned in no particular order.

Drill chucks
There is very little to say about the drill chuck, other than to purchase a good-quality item. Whilst this chuck is used mainly in the tailstock, it will occasionally find a use in the lathe's mandrel. This will not create a problem provided both have the same size taper, but some lathes have a different taper and a second chuck will be required. I do not put this in the same 'must have' category as the one for the tailstock

Centres
Headstock and tailstock centres are also essential but there have been some changes in their terminology, which I feel obliged to explain.

Starting with the situation that prevailed until quite recently, which some readers may still understand as the norm, centres were available in two forms, soft and hard, known respectively as "live" and "dead". The live centre was used in the lathe's mandrel and, because it rotated with

the workpiece, did not need to be hardened. This was not a money-saving ploy, but being soft, the centre could be turned in situ to ensure that it ran perfectly true at the start of each application. This is essential where precision is required when turning items between centres, particularly where the workpiece needs to be turned end on end during the machining process. The dead centre, being mounted in the tailstock, does not rotate and therefore needs to be hard or else it will wear rapidly.

Live (soft) centres are now conspicuously absent from present-day catalogues and I can only assume that the bore in modern lathes is now so much more accurate (concentric with its bearings) that the need for soft centres is a thing of the past. If you have an elderly lathe, or decide to purchase one, you may still have a need for a soft centre. Where you would obtain one may be a problem, and making your own is probably the best way out and not that difficult.

The present-day situation is slightly different. The term "dead centre" still applies to normal hard centres, intended for use in both the lathe's mandrel and the tailstock. However, the term "live centre" is now used for centres where the centre itself runs in bearings, allowing it to rotate with the workpiece; it is used in the lathe's tailstock (**Photo 16**). What are their advantages? Wear of the centre itself and the drilled centre in the workpiece will be minimal, but more importantly, the lack of friction will greatly reduce the amount of heat generated, and it is heat that causes the workpiece to expand. On the down side, the centre will be appreciably more expensive. Whether this expense is justifiable depends on the amount of between-centres work that you anticipate carrying out; it is certainly not an essential item.

The final common form of centre is the half centre, which is used when you need to face

16. This set-up uses a live centre that runs freely in its own bearings, thus generating less heat than a fixed centre.

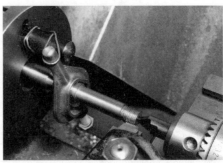

17. A catch plate and lathe dog being used to drive a part mounted between centres.

the end of a workpiece that is supported by the tailstock centre. In this case, it will be difficult to get the tool fully into the drilled centre impression and, as a result,a small portion of the end face will not be machined. This can be avoided by using a half centre that has had its end cut away, allowing the tool to fully machine the workpiece's end face. Although the device is called a half centre, it is actually more of a 5/8 centre because a small portion of the point remains fully round.

When working between centres, a normal centre can be used for the bulk of the work, with the half centre only being fitted for the final facing of the end. My approach to this has been to make a small half centre from hardened silver steel and, rather than making it with a Morse taper, to make it with a parallel shank that is then held in the drill chuck. This is more than adequate for the limited use it is likely to get.

Other types include large-diameter centres for supporting the inner wall of tubing, and reverse centres for supporting the outer rim, perhaps chamfered, of the workpiece. I have mentioned these for completeness but would not expect them to find a place in the average home workshop.

Catch plate and lathe dog

For the workpiece that is mounted between centres, some means of driving it must be provided. This is normally with a catch plate and a lathe dog, as shown in **Photo 17** (which also shows a half centre, as mentioned above). It would seem that catch plates are not provided for modern lathes, doubtless with the intention that the faceplate supplied should perform their function.

Tailstock die holders

Once a workpiece has been turned to the required diameter, it can be removed from the lathe and a thread produced on it using a manual diestock. With this method, it is not easy to get the thread to run perfectly in line and it is all but essential to carry out the threading operation on the lathe. This requires a tailstock-mounted die holder. The traditional approach to this was

18. A die holder in use on the lathe. It is a good idea to have a series of these already set up with the workshop's most used dies.

to mount a spindle on the tailstock's taper and then to mount the die holder on this, enabling it to be rotated manually, thus ensuring that the resulting thread was perfectly in line. The holder was then bored to accept 13/16in. dies at one end and 1in. dies at the other.

Photo 18 shows a variation on this, in which individual holders are used for each size of die. In fact, it is a good idea to have a holder ready set up and adjusted for each commonly used thread. To illustrate this, the photograph also shows a second holder, with a die fitted, resting on the top slide.

Steadies
These come in two forms: fixed and travelling.

Fixed steadies
I believe the fixed steady to be all but essential for the vast majority of workshops, but I fear that many workshop owners do not get the best from this very useful item. Its uses are many and varied and can only be described here in the briefest of detail. They can be divided into two groups.

The first, and essential, use for the fixed steady, is where a part is too long to be held just in the chuck and the outer end needs to be worked on, making it impossible to use the tailstock centre for support. The most common approach is first to carry out the bulk of the work while the workpiece is supported by the tailstock centre. With that done, the workpiece can be supported using the fixed steady and the centre can be removed. Machining the outer end can then be completed unhindered by the presence of the tailstock.

The second application is one that I feel is much under-used. Of course, being under-used does indicate that it is not essential for the task being undertaken. Sometimes, it is required to make a complete item from bar material without removing it from the chuck. If the material is too large to pass through the lathe's mandrel, a short stub will remain in the chuck after the part is parted off.

If a longer length of material is placed in the chuck and supported towards the end, the part can be made still leaving a reasonable length of material (Photo 19). Where required, the fixed steady can be moved towards the chuck to allow another part to be made. This process eliminates material wastage and is often worth adopting. The photograph shows a quantity of heavy-duty washers for use on the milling

19. A fixed steady is an essential accessory for use on the lathe.

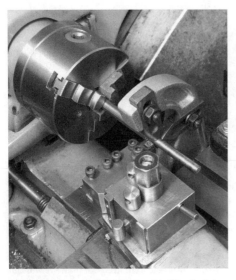

20. When turning long slender items, a travelling steady is essential.

21. Even if the outer end of the workpiece can be supported by the tailstock centre, a travelling steady may still be required to ensure that it does not become barrel shaped. It is essential in the case of the square thread leadscrew being made in this photograph.

machine being made requiring a lot of parting off. This is one of the most arduous tasks for a lathe and shows that the set-up is capable of heavy-duty work.

Travelling steadies

Travelling steadies are of limited use and many workshop owners will probably get by without one. However, where a definite need arises, any alternative method is likely to be far from satisfactory. For example, reducing a 12mm diameter to 6mm over a length of 25mm is an easy task; even over a length of 50mm, it would be possible taking light cuts with a sharp tool. However, beyond this length, the workpiece would bend and the resulting diameter would be larger at the outer end than at the chuck. In this case, a travelling steady would have to be used (**Photo 20**).

This problem could possibly be eliminated by supporting the outer end with the tailstock centre.

However, with extra-long lengths, the part would flex in the middle, creating a barrel shape. **Photo 21** shows a particularly crucial application where a square thread leadscrew is being made.

Knurling tools

Knurling is an operation that almost all workshop owners will need to carry out at some time, albeit infrequently, which is why I have included it in the "must have" category. There are two types of knurling tool, with variations within each group.

The simplest is a single-wheel tool that is applied to the workpiece to create the pattern required. This method exerts considerable force on the workpiece, and therefore on the bearings and leadscrews of the lathe itself, so it is not ideal.

On the other hand, the two-wheel tool (**Photo 22**) applies a wheel on either side of the part being knurled and, as a result, the loads largely cancel reach other out. This is therefore preferable for use on the lightweight machines found in most home workshops.

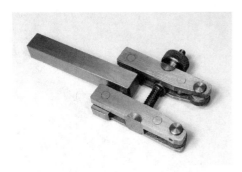

22. A two-wheel knurling tool is to be preferred because it balances the forces on the two wheels.

The wheels within the tool can be changed to produce either a straight knurl or a diamond knurl. A diamond knurl requires two wheels, so it can only easily be produced using the two-wheel tool. At this point, I should add that there are some two-wheel tools that enable diamond knurls to be made in which the wheels are close together. These have the same disadvantage as the single-wheel device.

In each type of knurling tool, there are wheels to produce knurls in a range of pitches, from fine to coarse; the purpose of the knurl will determine which to use.

Saddle stop

Whilst a saddle stop is not exactly an essential item, it makes many tasks so much easier that, for me, it comes into the "must have" category. Photo 23 shows a typical example being used to set the depth of a bore that is to be made in the workpiece. For many lathes, saddle stops are not available commercially, so it is a case of making one in the workshop.

Other accessories

The lathe is without doubt the most adaptable of the machine tools found in the home workshop, hence the large number of attachments that are

23. A saddle stop can be an advantage in a wide range of activities on the lathe.

available. There are too many to discuss fully here, but a few warrant a brief comment. From this, it should be obvious that they are in no way essential items for most workshops and it is a case of purchasing them if a need arises.

Tailstock Turret

When producing batches of identical parts, a tailstock turret can sometimes help to speed up the process. Typically, when parts need to be tapped in their end face, the turret can be set up with centre drill, drill and tap for immediate use and there will be no need to continually change the tools in a single drill chuck.

Back stop

Another item that is sometimes useful, especially when producing parts in batches, is a back stop. This is set up within the lathe's mandrel bore and enables parts to be returned to the chuck in exactly the same axial position for second operation work. Because of this, subsequent parts can be machined identically using the lathe's micrometer dials but without the need for measurements to be taken. To my knowledge, these are not available commercially so they will have to be shop made.

Coolant pump

The larger lathes are often equipped with a coolant pump, to cool and lubricate the cutting tool as machining is taking place, and thus extend the life of the tool. If one is already fitted to your machine, it would be reasonable to make use of the facility. However, a pump is by no means an essential feature for most workshop activities and, therefore, is not an item that needs to be added to a machine. Many workshop owners machine most things dry, using just a brush to add a little coolant when machining difficult materials, etc. and find this more than adequate.

Keats angle plate

This is rather like a large V block, but with lugs that enable it to be mounted on the lathe's faceplate (**Photo 24**). These plates are for holding round, square, and sometimes irregular, workpieces when they are too large for the 3- or 4-jaw chucks available. Another application is to set the part that is being machined off centre, so that non-concentric diameters can be produced. Whilst it is considered primarily as a device for mounting on the lathe's faceplate, it can also find use on the milling machine.

24. A Keats angle plate being used to hold a workpiece too large for the available chucks.

Non-turning operations
Boring

Even if you have opted to for a machine shop that includes a milling machine, there will be occasions when you will find it advantageous to carry out non-turning operations using the lathe, for example, boring a hole through a workpiece mounted onto the lathe's cross slide (**Photo 25**). In this case, the cutter is held in the 4-jaw, enabling it to be adjusted to suit the bore's required diameter by adjusting the chuck's jaws. A more advanced method is to use a boring head with a calibrated feed, making it easier to set. Boring heads are more frequently used on milling machines and are discussed in detail in Chapter 14.

Where the depth of bore is too great to be produced with an extended tool, a boring bar mounted between centres is normally used. In this case, the amount by which the tool projects from the bar governs the diameter being made. This needs some careful adjustment to obtain the required diameter. However, if one end is held in a 4-jaw chuck, very small adjustments can be made using this to arrive at the final diameter.

25. Even if a milling machine is available, it can sometimes be an advantage to use the lathe for non-turning applications.

26. A set-up for dividing on the lathe.

As using the 4-jaw requires no extra equipment, other than a simple tool holder, it is obviously the method to adopt initially. If a deeper hole is required, then a between centres bar is easily made in the workshop. Of course, a T-slotted cross slide is needed to secure the workpiece for carrying out these operations.

Dividing

It was the practice for many years to use the lathe as a means of dividing a workpiece for such operations as gear cutting, making a hexagon for a spanner, etc. Whilst the greater use of the milling machine now makes this less common, there are still operations where it is advantageous to use this method. If you have opted to work without a milling machine, then it will be the only method available. This

is a complex subject, and you will need to look elsewhere for advice, for example, Dividing (Workshop Practice Series Number 37).

The simplest method of establishing the divisions, although there are many others, is to mount a changewheel on the lathe's mandrel and use this together with a suitably mounted detent to set the divisions required. This facility is not available commercially and will need to be made in the workshop. **Photo 26** shows a typical example.

Chapter 12

The drilling machine and accessories

The drilling machine is probably the simplest of all the machines likely to be found in the home workshop and, as a result, it is probably not treated with the respect it deserves. It most certainly is not just a case of fitting the drill, placing the workpiece, pulling the lever and drilling a hole.

The machine
The first decision to be made when purchasing a drilling machine is its size in terms of drilling capacity. Here lies a real problem because, unfortunately, a machine's capacity is quoted in terms of the size of drill that the chuck will hold. Be warned that its ability to hold a 16mm drill is no indication that it will drill a 16mm hole in steel, even if a pilot hole is drilled first.

I would advise you against purchasing one of the very small machines (**Photo 1**), unless you anticipate working solely on very small-scale projects, although one can be a very useful as a back-up for a larger machine. At the other end of the scale, drilling a 16mm hole, even

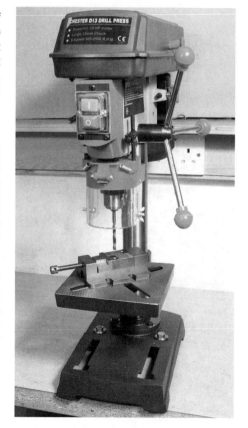

1. A small drilling machine is only suitable if you are working in the smallest scales or as a back-up to a larger machine.

after a 4mm pilot, will demand a substantial machine. As well as the capacity of the chuck, motor power, speed range and robustness all play an important role If you anticipate drilling a lot of large holes, say 12mm plus, then talk to a number of suppliers, giving exact details of your requirements; if you can visit them, ask for a demonstration.

2. A floor-mounted machine avoids the need for a deeper bench (as would be required for a bench-mounted machine). Also the greater chuck-to-worktable dimension can be a considerable advantage when mounting other items on the table.

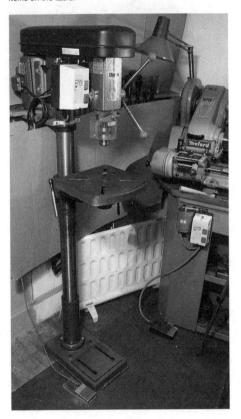

Mounting

Your next decision is whether the drill should be bench-mounted or floor-mounted. One feature of a bench-mounted drilling machine that can present a problem is its depth, which is the result of the overhanging motor at the rear; even a small machine can be too deep for the average bench. I have even seen the motor swung to the side of the machine to overcome this problem. An alternative is a floor-mounted version, which may be easier to site (**Photo 2**).

Another advantage of the floor-mounted version is the availability of a greater chuck-to-worktable dimension. This is worth serious consideration, especially if you expect to add items to the worktable that will reduce the available height, typically a cross vice, or even a compound table.

Speed range

The drilling machine's speed range is also a very important consideration because you are likely to use a wide range of drill sizes. In theory, a drill size range of 1mm to 16mm requires a speed range of around 2500 rpm down to 150 rpm. In addition, there should be at least ten fixed speeds within this range; the five fixed speeds frequently provided are certainly not ideal. If your intended activity involves a lot of drilling at the smaller sizes, say below 2mm, then the top speed is very important. Attempting to drill a small hole at too low a speed is a recipe for broken drills and you should aim for a top speed of 3000 rpm, or even higher if you envisage drilling holes of less than 1mm.

You should also check the speeds provided because they are not always what you might expect. My 16-speed machine, with a range of 180 rpm to 2700 rpm, would seem ideal but, as I found out too late, there is an interval of 680 rpm to 1170 rpm in the middle of the range – nearly 2:1, which is ridiculous!

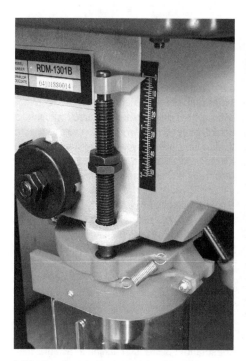

3. This down-feed stop arrangement provides a fine adjustment and is best for setting exact depths, typically when countersinking. However, it is slow to set.

4. The photograph shows a more rapidly set down-feed stop. Although adequate for most requirements, it is much more difficult to achieve a precise result using this method.

Other features

Other features include a depth stop and a tilting table. In the case of the depth stop, some machines are provided with a fine adjustment that uses a nut running up and down a threaded rod (**Photo 3**), but, in others, the adjustment will be less precise (**Photo 4**). However, the depth of holes drilled is rarely crucial, so either will suit for most operations, but the less precise method is certainly much quicker to set. Some tasks, however, such as countersinking to a given diameter, are more demanding in terms of drilled depth. In this case, the fine adjustment would be an advantage but is by no means essential.

The ability to tilt the table to enable holes to be drilled at an angle in the workpiece can be useful, although it is probably easier to use a tilting vice or some other means. This is because there is no fine adjustment, so returning the table to a position at right angles to the drill is not that easy and is very much a case of trial and error. How to make this adjustment has already been described in detail in the chapter on machine installation (Chapter 9).

Controls

This subject, being very largely applicable to all power tools, has already been covered in Chapter 8. However, I would reiterate that a no-volt release starter, together with a foot switch

5. As you are likely to be using both hands when a drilling problem arises, a foot switch is an essential safety feature.

(**Photo 5**), should be considered essential in the case of a drilling machine, which has very specific safety considerations (see "Vices", below).

Accessories

Many of the accessories used with a drilling machine can also be used with other machines, in some cases predominantly with one particular machine. Consequently, I will discuss these items in full under the headings of the machine where they are most used, giving only a passing comment under other machine tool headings.

Drills

As mentioned in the chapter on workshop planning (Chapter 4), I would urge readers to use metric size drills because of the logical increments between sizes.

Whatever your preferred units, metric or imperial, there is still a wide range of drills to choose from, although most are very specialised and found only in the catalogues of suppliers to industry. Even so, if you purchase from those who supply predominantly to the home workshop, the choice is still more than adequate for the vast majority of the tasks that you are likely to undertake.

Jobber drills

By far the most common are the standard length drills sharpened to a point angle of 118°, frequently referred to as "jobber drills". You may also occasionally find a use for a long-series drill with a flute length of about twice that of the jobber drill. You are unlikely to purchase a complete set but a few common values will do to start with; alternatively, purchase as required. Even longer drills are available, but these are definitely "buy as required" items!

Blacksmith drills

Another fairly common drill form is the blacksmith drill. These are large-size drills, say 25mm, but with a shank size of 12mm. This enables you to use drills larger than the chuck's capacity. Even so, do not be fooled into thinking that you will be able to drill 25mm holes in steel on your average home-workshop drilling machine. It may just be possible, by opening up the hole in stages, but you will need a slow speed and a powerful machine to achieve this. However, it is useful to have two or three sizes for use on the lathe as they are generally more robust and powerful than a drilling machine. In this situation, they will enable a large hole to be drilled prior to final boring to a larger hole size.

Stub drills

You may also find stub drills listed in catalogues. These have shorter flutes than jobber drills and, as a result, are more robust. This makes them ideal for use in a handheld pistol drill, although they are of limited use in the workshop. You may find a use for them when drilling difficult materials or, occasionally, if you have insufficient headroom in your machine, purchasing a stub drill just for a particular job may get you out of a difficult situation.

Countersinks

It may be a temptation to use a large drill instead of a countersink when countersinking

6. The photograph shows a single and a three-flute countersink (front left) and a multi-flute countersink (front right). Also shown are some counterbores: shop-made rear (rear left) and commercially available (rear right).

Counterbores

Also shown in **Photo 6** are some counterbores (shop-made, rear left, and commercial items rear right). These are mainly used to drill flat-bottomed holes to take the head of a socket cap screw and include a pilot to locate in the pre-drilled hole for the screw eventually to be fitted. Because of this, the clearance hole size must be a close fit on the pilot. If you have some silver steel available and wish to hone your hardening skills, you may like to make your own, but modern-day versions are not that expensive so it is debatable whether this is worthwhile.

Vice

You may think that the drilling machine and the cutters to drill the holes are all that you require. Unfortunately, some people adopt this attitude and attempt to handhold the workpiece. Do **not** do this because it is extremely dangerous! It may be acceptable in a few cases, typically drilling small holes in large workpieces, but some mechanical help in holding the part is invariably necessary. This can most often be achieved by using a vice.

If a vice is available, it may be sufficient to handhold it in place but, again, this will depend on circumstances. A small component in a large vice is the equivalent of a large workpiece and, if the hole being drilled is small, say 5mm or less, handholding the vice will be acceptable – but I would emphasise the word **large** in terms of the vice.

Above this size, or even smaller in the case of difficult materials, the vice should be clamped firmly to the machine table. This is because, if the drill seizes in the hole being drilled, the vice may be pulled from your hand and rotate dangerously. Even worse, as the drill breaks through, it may attempt to rise up the drill's flute and, if removed from your grasp, will rotate

for a countersunk screw, but the difference in angle makes this far from ideal: with a metric screw having an internal angle of 90° and the drill an angle of 118°, the difference is too great to make it acceptable. However, if you have a drill-sharpening attachment that can sharpen to angles other than 118°, it may be acceptable. Even so, countersinks are not that expensive, and only one is required, so there seems to be little point in going down the road of a modified drill.

As **Photo 6** shows, there are a several different types to choose from, including single and three-flute sinks (front left) and the multi-flute sink (front right). The larger one, which just has a hole through the head, is sometimes called a zero flute. This is often referred to as a hole deburring tool, a task that it does well, even when handheld. Even so, some catalogues give it the status of a countersink bit. The multi-flute sink is inclined to chatter more than the others, so I would not recommend it. Any of the other three is worth trying.

7. A drilling vice is an essential item but there is a wide range from which to choose. The photograph shows a very good-quality vice (top) and a budget-quality vice (bottom).

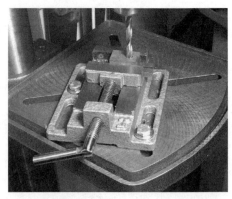

8. The advantage of the budget-quality vice is its longer fixings, which make it easier to fasten to the machine table.

violently above the table's surface. At best, you are likely to have a broken drill; at worst, you will be on your way to hospital. The above comments also apply when the component itself is being handheld during drilling.

In my opinion, the drilling machine's potential for injury is very much underestimated. As I commented at the beginning of this chapter, the drilling machine is a simple machine to use, which may lead to complacency. It is because of its dangers that I have stressed that a foot switch should be an essential part of the machine's control system. There are occasions where the drilling process starts to get a little out of hand and, whilst not dangerous at that stage, the operator is reluctant to let go of either the workpiece or the down-feed handle. In such cases, the foot switch can be a disaster stopper!

Having established that a drilling machine vice is essential, there are a large number advertised specifically for this purpose. Photo 7 shows two: a very good-quality vice (top), which is not overly expensive and could also be used on the milling machine for many tasks, and a budget-quality vice (bottom). In my opinion,

the better-quality vice is more suited to milling whereas the budget-quality vice has one major advantage: greater flexibility for securing it to the machine table.

The better-quality vice has only two short fixing slots, and it may not always be possible to align these slots with the slots in the machine table at the same time as aligning the drill with the position required. On the other hand, **Photo 8** shows how the four long slots in the budget-quality vice make it easily possible to find a suitable clamping position. This makes it more likely that the operator will clamp the vice to the table rather than handhold it, which is a definite safety bonus.

Whilst the above will provide a very safe working situation, it is not ideal, as the vice will need repositioning for every hole drilled, which may deter the operator from clamping the vice in place. In many cases, this can be overcome by using a cross vice, as shown in **Photo 9**. This has dovetail slides and feed screws in both the X- and the Y- axis, enabling the workpiece to be lined up for all the holes within the range of the vice's traverse. The one

10. A compound table is the ultimate in terms of convenience and makes using a drilling machine much easier

9. Using a cross vice avoids the need to reposition the vice on the machine table for each hole drilled.

11. A dividing head will sometimes find a use on the drilling machine and, whilst this one is shown on a compound table, it can also be mounted directly onto the machine's table.

shown in the photograph is 75mm, but, except for use on one of the very small machines, I would recommend a larger version, say at least 100mm, with traverses of around 60mm and 80mm. Of course, you will need to ensure that your machine has sufficient headroom to cope with the height of the cross vice: 140mm in the case of a 100mm vice.

Close examination of **Photo 9** will show that the lower operating handle has been extended because it invariably fouls the machine's table; this entails a relatively simple modification.

Compound table

A compound table (**Photo 10**) is the ultimate in terms of convenience and makes using a drilling machine so much easier. The photograph shows that the better of the two vices shown in Photo 7 has been added to the end of the table, for use as required. However, by mounting it off centre, a generous area is still available for mounting other items, typically, a dividing head (**Photo 11**) or a large workpiece (**Photo 12**). Note how, in this photograph, a

short clamp has been fixed to the machine table to go under the workpiece before adding a top clamp. This raises the workpiece, thus ensuring that the drill will avoid the table as it breaks through. With traverse values of 280mm and 155mm, the table is adequate for all but the largest workpieces.

My earlier comment regarding headroom is equally applicable here, with the compound table having a height of 125mm, even before adding the dividing head. In this case, however, of even greater importance is the weight of the

12. A large workpiece being drilled using the compound table to position each required hole.

table (24kg), which will need a fairly substantial machine on which to mount it. In addition, with so much added weight at the front of the machine, the machine must be firmly anchored. In the case of a relatively light-duty floor-mounted machine, it is a good idea to make a bracket to fix the column to the workshop wall just below the machine's head. If you have a lighter duty machine then all is not lost because smaller compound tables are available.

These tables, as well as the cross vices, are often advertised as being capable of light milling operations. This is not the case because a drilling machine has no fine down feed and no method of clamping it in any position. In addition, a drill chuck is by no means suitable for holding milling cutters. Nevertheless, in an extreme case, I suppose it might be possible to set the drilling machine's downfeed stop and hold the down feed firmly against it with one hand whilst your other hand traverses the table – but this is not really a practical idea! I make this point to ensure that you do not go down the road of purchasing a compound table thinking that this will avoid the need to purchase a milling machine.

While I regard a compound table as a luxury for most workshops, I consider cross vices, which are remarkably cheap, to be essential on both safety and convenience grounds.

Other accessories
Occasionally, it may be preferable to use an angle plate instead of a vice for holding a workpiece. In this case, clamping the part to the angle plate and the angle plate to the table is similar to its use on a milling machine.

V blocks are another item that may find a use on the machine table but here the situation is more complex: first and foremost there is no easy way of fixing them into place. Probably the easiest way out of this problem is to use one, or maybe two, V blocks held in a vice. Unless you can provide some means of firmly clamping the workpiece, you should only use a V block when drilling small holes.

Using a drilling machine
Using a drilling machine is mostly a matter of common sense. As already mentioned, securely anchoring the workpiece for drilling is essential except for smaller holes. The next consideration is drill speed. Fortunately, drill speed is not crucial, but it is important to understand that a high speed is needed for small drills, or else they may break. For larger drills, the set-up will complain if the speed is too great, particularly if, rather than drilling the hole in one go, you attempt to open it up from a smaller size, when chatter is a likely result.

It is important to keep your drills sharp, a subject that is discussed in Chapter 15. It is also advisable to use a cutting lubricant when drilling more difficult materials, such as copper, stainless steel, etc.

After marking out the position of the hole to be drilled using two scribed lines, you should centre punch the workpiece at this point to guide the drill into the correct position. For this to work well, the diameter of the centre punch mark must be larger than the length of the chisel point of the drill. For larger drills, this needs to be quite large, and starting the hole with a small centre drill is a good approach. Where the accuracy of position is not that critical, you may even start the hole without centre punching when using a centre drill.

***

Probably the most common milling machine now in use in the average home workshop is the so-called mill/drill (see Chapter 13). This is really no more than a substantial drilling head with a fine down feed, equipped with a heavy-duty compound table.

In theory, a mill/drill machine could meet all your drilling requirements and, if the disadvantages are acceptable, your workshop could function without a machine designed specifically for drilling.

In my opinion, the major problem with mill/drill machines is the frequent need to break down the milling set-up on the machine table in order to enable drilling operations to be carried out. The constant addition and removal of items such as vices, angle plates, and milling cutter chucks for drill chucks would eventually become too much of a chore. The heavy-duty head, together with an insufficiently high top speed, would also make drilling small holes impractical. On the plus side, the machine, being robust, would be ideal for drilling those large holes that are at the limit of the available drilling machine's capacity.

Chapter 13

The milling machine

Unlike the lathe, where the only major differences are size, quality and price, milling machines are much more variable in terms of design. The major difference is in the orientation of the cutter's spindle: vertical or horizontal. The vertical machine has similarities to a drilling machine and uses cutters called "end mills"; these are not that different from a twist drill but, despite their name, they cut predominantly on their side. Horizontal mills use cutters called "side and face cutters", which are rather like a very substantial circular saw blade. Photo 1 shows examples of end mills (left), a side and face cutter (centre) and slot drills (right and rear). Most side and face cutters are much wider than the one shown

1. End mills (left), side and face cutter (centre) and slot drills (right and rear).

When it comes to choosing the type of machine with which to equip your workshop, there is really only one answer: a vertical mill. This is by far the best option for almost all milling operations. However, there are many versions of the vertical mill and the choice is far from easy. However, the method by which they are used will be virtually the same whichever one is chosen, and it will be much simpler than any of the wide range of tasks undertaken on a lathe.

Turret mills

At the top end of the range are the turret mills (**Photo 2**). These are primarily industrial machines but, at the lower end of the size range, may fit into the home workshop budget for some. Their main feature, and a distinct advantage over others, is that the three axes, X, Y and Z (**see Sk. 1**), are all provided by means of dovetail slides moving the table. In non-technical terms, these are left/right, towards/away and up/down. The part of the machine that provides the up/down movement (Z) is often referred to as the knee.

The head is similar to that of a drilling machine, although it is built to a very much higher standard and with a calibrated vertical feed. When added to the up/down table movement, this provides a wide range of cutter-to-table

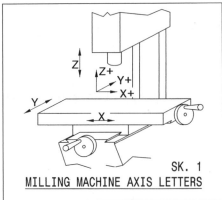

SK. 1
MILLING MACHINE AXIS LETTERS

2. A very well-equipped turret mill. This is fitted with digital read-out and power feeds, although these are normally options rather than standard. Table size is 152 × 660mm. (Warco).

dimensions, enabling tool changes without losing position (see "Mill/Drills" below). In addition to the fine down feed, they can also be lever operated, enabling drilling operations to be carried out. A major advantage of using the machine for drilling is that hole centres can be very accurately set by reference to the table's X and Y micrometer dials, so there is no need for marking out. Although they are at the more expensive end of home workshop mills, they are not necessarily the machines with the largest capacity; some mill/drills have larger tables and traverse. Changing speed will be by belt, gears, or electronic controls.

Mill/Drills

The other machines are those in which the table provides only the X- and Y-axis while the Z-axis is provided by moving the head up and down and the spindle up and down within the head.

There is considerable variation in these machines but probably the most common are the so-called mill/drills (**Photo 3**). These have a head almost the equal of a drilling machine head but more robust and with a calibrated down feed in addition to the lever feed for drilling. There is also provision for locking the down feed in place while a cut is being taken. The head is mounted on a round column, on which it moves up and down to provide the main adjustment for the distance between the head and table. On most machines, there is no calibration on this feature, which is used only to roughly position the head; the final positioning of the cutter is by means of the spindle's fine feed within the head. Although this works well for most tasks, it has one major weakness that may occasionally cause a problem.

For ease of explanation, I will take the simple example of drilling a large hole. If you first use a short centre drill to establish the position of the hole, you will find it necessary to raise the head to fit the much longer drill. As the column is

3. A typical mill/drill with a table size of 190 × 585mm (Chester).

round, the head will probably rotate a little on the column as it is raised. If this happens, the drill will not align with the pre-drilled centre. Similarly, if you are attempting to accurately machine a complex part at different levels relative to each other, then any loss of position will make the process more difficult. Fortunately, for the vast majority of the applications, this problem will not arise, particularly if care is taken to avoid it by starting with the most suitable table- to-head distance.

Within limits, the ability to rotate the head on the round column can be a benefit because it will enable the cutter to reach parts of the table that would not be available with a fixed head. Again, this will be an infrequent requirement so is not a major consideration.

In a variation on the original mill/drill format, the round column is replaced with a dovetail slide so that register is maintained as the head is raised

and lowered. Because of this, the up/down feed may be calibrated, although this is often not done as the movement of the spindle within the head still provides this essential feature.

Like the turret mills, the mill/drills and their variants may have belt, geared or electronic speed control.

Common features
Speed control
As already commented on, speed control can be provided by belt change, geared head or an electronic control. Machines using belts will be among the cheapest, but changing the position of the belts on the pulleys can be a chore, tempting you to work at a less than ideal speed. Geared heads, on the other hand, provide simple and very quick speed change (while the drive is stationary, of course), but are more expensive and can be noisy. Electronic controls have advantages and disadvantages but, as these are common to all machines, the subject is discussed in general terms in Chapter 8.

Speed ranges
Speed requirements follow the usual pattern: small cutters, high speed; large cutters, low speed. Unfortunately, once you have made your decision regarding the size and type of the machine for your workshop, there will not be a lot of scope for choosing the speeds you require. Even so, the speed ranges on most milling machines are reasonably adequate, certainly more so than with the lathe.

Whilst most of the work carried out on a milling machine, typically surfacing and making rebates, can be carried out with the same size end mill, say 16mm, there are times when smaller cutters need to be used. This is most likely when slots, enclosed or otherwise, are being made. If these are small, say 3mm, then a speed in the order of 2000 rpm plus should be sought.

When using a 20mm end mill on steel, a speed of 300 rpm is ideal. However, intermittent cuts, using, say, a 50mm face cutter on cast iron, will demand lower speeds. For this, speeds as low as 100 rpm would be beneficial but, at these speeds, the robustness of the machine becomes an important factor.

As a rule of thumb, I would advise a speed range of 100–2000 rpm for a typical mill/drill. If you are limited to a lighter weight machine, then a minimum speed of, say, 300–400 rpm should suffice, as it will not be expected to carry out heavy-duty tasks. Small diameters will still be likely, perhaps more so, so a top speed of 2000 rpm is still preferable.

If you consider a machine with an electronic control that quotes a speed range of, say, 0–2000 rpm, do be suspicious of the zero figure. The machine may just be able to run at a few rpm (I have my doubts) but, at such a speed, the power available will be equally low and insufficient to perform any useful work. It is often at the lower speeds that the most demands are placed on the machine, so do find out the minimum speed at which the machine will function satisfactorily.

Rotating head

Some machines have the facility to rotate the head (i.e. clockwise/anticlockwise as you view the machine from the front), enabling the cutter to approach the table at an angle, but how useful this will be depends on the machine's intended use. Even if this facility is available, I suspect that it will rarely be used, if ever, so it is far from essential. Once the head has been angled, returning it accurately to the normal working position is a similar but even more demanding task than that described for setting a drilling machine's tilting table because much greater accuracy is essential if end mills and slot drills are to cut as intended. This requirement

for accuracy alone would be a deterrent from using the head at an angle unless there was no other option.

Calibrated X, Y and Z feeds

All three axes will have calibrated micrometer dials, enabling the amount of feed to be accurately set. Early machines, and possibly still some at the economy end of the price range, had fixed dials. With a fixed dial, after making the cut, measuring the result and determining the amount that still needs to be removed, some mental arithmetic is necessary to determine the dial setting required to achieve the depth of cut. However, if the dial can be zeroed, it is a case of just zeroing the dial and setting it to the depth of cut required. This is therefore a highly desirable feature.

Digital read-outs

These devices are sometimes fitted for use in addition to the micrometer dials but are presently only available on more expensive and mostly industrial machines. Even here, a digital read-out is frequently an option rather than a standard fitment. Although equipment for adding this facility to existing machines is widely available, there is no standard as far as machine design is concerned and therefore no standard method of fitting these. Because of this, you will need to determine your own method should you decide to add them yourself. **Photo 4** shows a digital read-out fitted to the down feed on a mill/drill. This was fitted because vibration caused the poorly balanced operating handle, and therefore the micrometer dial, to rotate while a cut was being taken, making it difficult to place on another cut with any degree of accuracy.

Traverse stops

These are very useful where an operation has to be carried out repeatedly over a given range, either on a single component or for batch

4. A digital read-out added to a mill/drill's down feed.

5. As Y-axis stops are rarely available on machines as purchased, shop-made stops, like those shown in this photograph are the only option. Note the right-hand X-axis stop and the stop bar which it contacts to stop the table.

production. A typical example is the need to machine a slot with closed ends, which requires the table to be traversed over the same distance each time the cutter is dropped deeper into the slot being made. Setting the table stops will make this operation much easier than relying on reading the micrometer dials to establish the end positions at each pass.

These stops appear to be standard on the average size mill/drill and larger, but not on the smaller machines, which is a pity. Table stops for the Y-axis are not normally provided, even on more expensive machines. However, needing to mill an enclosed recess to a depth of around 12mm, I decided to fit Y-axis stops of my own design, as **Photo 5** shows. Although useful, this gets far less use than the X-axis

stops, which I consider to be almost essential. The photograph also shows the right hand X-axis stop and the stop bar which it contacts to stop the table.

Down feed (Z) stops are useful, typically when drilling blind holes to a given depth. Like X-axis stops, these do not seem to be included on most of the smaller machines although they are standard on mill/drills of average size and larger. A typical example of a down feed to the right of the digital read-out is shown in **Photo 4**.

Power feed

Another feature limited to the X-axis, except on

some very expensive machines, is a power feed, although, even on the X-axis, it is still an extra in most cases. While far from an essential, it is a useful feature if you do a lot of work surfacing large areas. Be warned though; the cost will be in the region of one third of the cost of the complete mill. Also, if you want to fit one to an existing machine you may need to carry out some minor modifications beforehand.

Draw bar

With the drilling machine, the pressure on the end of the drill is attempting to push the taper of the chuck into its mating taper; this is not the case with a milling cutter chuck. As mentioned above, end mills cut mainly on their side and, as a result, the spiral cutting edge attempts to draw the chuck from its taper. The intermittent cutting action also causes some vibration, which, together with the spiral effect, may remove the chuck from its socket, with potentially serious results. To prevent this, the end of the chuck's taper is threaded and a threaded bar is placed into it. This passes completely through the spindle and is tightened at the top in order to secure the chuck and prevent the problem.

A number of standard thread sizes are in use, mainly metric on metric machines and imperial threads on imperial machines, but as thread size tends to be linked to the size of the taper there is not normally a problem. However, if you have a metric machine but decide to purchase an imperial cutter chuck to use with existing cutters, you may find the Morse taper will have an imperial thread. Fortunately, all is not lost, because the draw bar is removable and an imperial threaded bar can easily be made and fitted. There may be just one problem with larger machines: the draw bars can be quite long and

there may be insufficient headroom for them to be interchanged easily.

Because of the spiral nature of the cutter's cutting edge any attempt to withdraw the chuck from its taper will also draw the cutter from the chuck. This situation is discussed later (see Chapter 14).

Spindle taper

At one time, there were other tapers in addition to Morse tapers, but these have been largely relegated to history, although you may come across them if you purchase an old secondhand machine. (Even here, I think this mainly applied to tapers on lathes.) Tapers have therefore become standardised on Morse tapers and a modern taper known as an R8 taper, although others are used on larger industrial machines.

The R8 taper was mainly used on industrial machines but is now found in larger machines in the home workshop. Morse tapers have been made in a large number of sizes over the years, but only three are likely to be found in the home workshop: mostly numbers 2 and 3 but occasionally number 1. The R8 taper is a single-size device and is quite large, which is why it only appears on larger machines (see Chapter 11, Photo 13).

Horizontal/Vertical attachments

These are available for a small number of industrial machines, enabling, say, a vertical machine to be converted into a horizontal machine, and vice versa. A few of the early very small industrial milling machines, still relatively common secondhand, had these attachments but, other than this, they are unlikely to be found in the average home workshop.

Chapter 14

Milling machine accessories

Once you have obtained your milling machine, there is still a wide range of accessories that can be added to it, a few of which are essential. Topping the list of essentials are two items: the cutters and, equally essential, a chuck designed to hold them. The drill chuck supplied with many mill/drills just will not do! In simple terms, the cutters come in two types: those that include a shank, by which they are held, and disk-shaped cutters that are held using the central hole.

Cutters with shanks

The non-working end

These cutters come in a wide range of types and sizes but at the non-working end, the shank, there are commonly only three. The least common are cutters that mount directly into the machine's taper, Morse or R8. These cutters are not solid high-speed steel (HSS) or carbide but have a normal steel shank, perhaps hardened, and removable tips.

One-piece solid cutters come with one of two parallel shank forms: plain, possibly with a flat for the use of a holding screw, or with a threaded end. The thread is the same diameter as the shank and has a 20 TPI Whitworth-form thread, even on metric cutters. The benefits and disadvantages of these forms are discussed below. Both types are shown in Chapter 13, Photo 1.

The working end

Indexable cutters

Removable tip (or indexable) cutters have tips that can be replaced when they become blunt. The holders can only accept one particular size and shape of tip, but they can be fitted with tips made from different grades of material and with minor changes in detail, such as the radius between cutting edges. However, in the home workshop, the general-purpose tip supplied with the holder when purchased will be suitable.

In most cases, each tip will have three or four cutting edges that can be moved to the next cutting position as use dictates and before a completely new tip is fitted. A few are fitted with round tips that can be rotated. **Photo 1** shows some commercially available, parallel shank cutters that I have myself permanently fitted into Morse taper shanks. Although shop-made, they are essentially the same as those available commercially. Some have just two tips, but

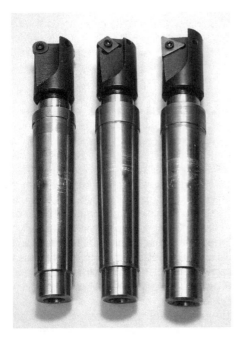

1. Indexable milling cutters with round (left), diamond (centre) and triangular (right) tips.

2. As this photograph shows, it is impossible to plunge the normal end mill because it does not cut to the cutter's centre

versions with three or four tips are available in larger sizes. A few of the smaller sizes, perhaps with just a single tip, have parallel shanks for holding a chuck.

Invariably the helix angle at the cutting edge is less than that on the solid HSS end mills and, on some, is even negative. For a given diameter, this results in a greater load on the machine using it. Because of this, they are not ideal for use on lightweight machines, say, those smaller than the average mill/drill. However, they are particularly suitable for machining iron castings because they are less affected by any hard spots that may occur.

Solid cutters
One-piece cutters are most frequently made

of HSS, but cutters made of carbide are also available, although their use is largely industrial. There are just two common forms of cutter: end mills and slot drills (see Chapter 13, Photo 1). The end mill is a general-purpose cutter capable of surfacing horizontal and vertical surfaces, machine steps and open-ended grooves.

Close examination of the end of the end mill shows that the four cutting edges do not go to the centre because there is a cavity in the centre. Consequently, the cutter cannot be plunged into a surface because it will not cut to the centre, as shown in **Photo 2**. Therefore, a slot drill is used when a closed end slot is required. This has one short and one long cutting edge, which pass through the centre,

3. Mini mills are can be plunged and are used primarily for milling closed end slots and open-ended grooves.

enabling it to be plunged and making it possible to machine enclosed slots. A few end mills are now being made without the cavity and can therefore be plunged, but whether they will eventually become standard only time will tell. However, they are much more difficult to sharpen than those with an end cavity.

Photo 3 shows some smaller end mills with three cutting edges. These are known as mini mills or, because they are not intended to be sharpened, throw-away mills. They can be plunged, with their main purpose being to machine open-ended grooves and closed end slots. They have a 6mm (or 1/4in.) diameter shank and a minimum size of 1.5mm (or 1/16in.). Ideally, you need a very high speed to use the smaller sizes, preferably at least 3000 rpm.

Which size?
In theory, only one size of end mill will be required because these mills are not intended to cut at their full width, except perhaps for very shallow surfacing. In normal practice, the width of cut should not exceed a nominal one-third of the cutter's diameter. Typically, this means 3mm when using an 8mm diameter cutter, or 5mm when using a 16mm diameter cutter. To minimise the number of passes necessary to machine a given width, a larger diameter will obviously be an advantage. Therefore, two

sizes are a good starting point; say 8mm and 10mm for smaller mills, 10mm and 16mm for an average size mill/drill, and 12mm and 20mm for a large machine.

For me, the quantity of each size is more important than the size itself. Without doubt, sharpening end mills and slot drills is the most demanding sharpening task undertaken in the average home workshop, taking an appreciable amount of time to set up, no matter what equipment is available for the task. Therefore, it is a good idea to have a quantity of each size so that you can delay sharpening operations until you have sufficient cutters needing sharpening to warrant setting up for the task. With this in mind, I would suggest a minimum of three of each size used. This will still be appropriate, even if you use a commercial firm for your end-mill sharpening requirements, although this is probably not economic except for the larger sizes.

The situation with slot drills is more complex because a single drill will only suffice for one width of slot. A slot is often used in combination with a screw, which passes through it to enable the position of one part to adjusted relative to another. On this basis, the screw sizes likely to be used will set the sizes of the slot drills to be obtained. Thus, for metric sizes of screw, say M5, M6, M8 and M10, slot drills of 5mm, 6mm, 8mm and 10mm will be required. However, you may choose to make your purchases as and when required. Even so, I would still recommend purchasing two of each size. (I suggest two rather than three because slot drills are likely to get much less use than end mills.)

Plain or threaded?
Shanks are either plain or threaded, but my overwhelming preference is for the threaded form, which I recommend you to adopt. The

4. Four types of milling cutter: (from left to right) T-slot cutter, ball-nosed end mill, rounding end mill, dovetail cutter. These should only be purchased as the need arises.

reasons for this are discussed when holding methods are considered (see below).

Other types

While the above will certainly satisfy virtually all your milling requirements, a few other cutters may be required, four of which are shown in **Photo 4**. The T-slot cutter (left) is the only means of machining T slots, should the need arise. Likewise, a special dovetail cutter (right) is the best means of machining dovetails. Both T-slots and dovetails can be machined quite easily using a shaper and simple cutters, but shaping machines are rarely found in the home workshop these days.

Another form of cutter has a curved end known as a ball end (**Photo 4**, centre left). These are sometimes called slot drills and at other times end mills; I do not know whether there is a difference but they both normally have just two flutes. Obviously, they can be used for milling grooves with a rounded bottom and, with care, no doubt, a step with a fillet between the horizontal and vertical surfaces. In industry, they are also used for machining complex

5. Disk-type cutters mounted on adapters to enable them to be used on a vertical machine: slitting saws (left), gear cutters (right).

shapes using computerised machines, a task required in only a very few home workshops.

Finally, as far as the home workshop is concerned, there are the rounding end mills (**Photo 4**, right of centre). These are used for producing an external radius between vertical and horizontal surfaces.

As the need for these four types of cutter is unpredictable, it is a case of purchasing them when they are required. Like many items in the workshop, many variations are available, and cutters are no exception. However, the cutters described above will be sufficient in all but the most exceptional cases, others being solely for use in the industrial world.

Disk-type cutters

These are intended primarily for use on

horizontal milling machines but, in their smaller sizes, are perfectly at home on the vertical mill, providing a suitable adapter is available. The adapter can have either a Morse or an R8 taper for direct fitting or, for smaller sizes, a parallel shank for use with the cutter chuck available (**Photo 5**). Cutters of this type are likely to be of limited use, with two common exceptions: slitting saws (left) and gear cutters (right).

Slitting saws come in two forms. Smaller sizes are flat with no set on their teeth and come in two pitches, fine and coarse, fine being about a 3mm pitch and coarse about 8mm. They are made in a wide range of diameters and thicknesses but only two bore sizes are common: 5/8in. and 1in. This limits the number of holding mandrels required. Heavy-duty slitting saws come in the form of a side and face cutter (see Chapter 13, Photo 1).

Gear cutters are likely to find a use in at least some home workshops, although probably not to the same extent as slitting saws. Unfortunately, even for a single gear-tooth size, be it DP (imperial) or MOD (metric), the shape of the tooth space varies depending on the number of teeth on the gear. In theory, therefore, the shape of the space is different for each number of teeth. However, as the difference is very small, a compromise shape is adopted so that each cutter will cover a range as follows:

Cutter number		Number of teeth cut	
DP	MOD	Minimum	Maximum
1	8	135	Rack
2	7	55	134
3	6	35	54
4	5	26	34
5	4	21	25
6	3	17	20 ·
7	2	14	16
8	1	12	13

The cutters are not sold in sets so it is possible to purchase them individually to meet your own requirements. These are definitely "purchase as required" items. Note that metric cutters are numbered in reverse order to imperial cutters.

Cutter holders

Apart from those that have their own taper shank, cutters need some additional means of holding them in the machine, and it is vital to have the correct equipment for this. In Chapter 13, it was explained how the cutter's helix can attempt to draw it from its mating taper, making a draw bar necessary. In the same way, the helix can attempt to draw a parallel shank cutter from the chuck that is holding it. Because of this, it is essential that the cutter is held in a suitable holder, because a drill chuck will most certainly not do this.

There are two methods of holding cutters: a simple holder and a collet chuck. The disadvantage of the holder is that it will only hold a single shank size, so typically four will be required: 6mm, 10mm, 12mm and 16mm, or the imperial equivalents. As collet chucks are now more reasonably priced, it is hardly worthwhile to purchase four holders.

Cutters come with either a plain shank (perhaps with a flat for a screw if it is held in a holder) or a threaded end. While there are chucks specific for each type, threaded shank cutters can be used in the chucks intended for plain shanks. However, if you do this, you lose the benefit that the threaded shank provides.

In the case of the threaded shank system, the collets used have a thread in the base to accept the thread on the shank but also have a through hole so that the centre impression on the end of the cutter can engage with a centre point in the base of the chuck. This ensures that the end is central in the chuck body. However, there is another more important aspect of this provision.

The tapered end of the collet used in this system has a large angle and, because of this, it is unable to convert efficiently the turning force of the closing ring into a sufficient gripping force. However, if the cutter rotates a little in the collet when a cut is being taken, it will not screw the cutter further into the chuck because it is already firmly in contact with the centre point in the base. The result, therefore, is to jack the collet forward into its closing ring, increasing the grip of the cutter. This alone will not prevent the cutter from rotating further because the increased friction between the cutter and the centre point and, more importantly, between the thread on the cutter and the thread in the collet, all contribute to the cutter not turning further.

With this method, the axial position of the cutter cannot change whatever the load placed on it because it will always remain firmly against the centre in the base. This is the major advantage of this type of milling cutter chuck and is the reason for its popularity. However, mini mills do not have a threaded shank, so if you wish to use one for machining narrow-width slots, you will need to make or purchase an adapter for use with this type of chuck. A major advantage of this form of chuck is that it can be tightened by hand, although a spanner may be required if a heavy cut has been taken.

For a collet solely to grip the cutter, it must have a small internal angle to convert the rotation of the closing ring into a grip sufficient to hold the cutter. Collets that meet this requirement are now more readily available and, to a small extent, have diminished the advantage of the collets described above. Even so, they do not have the same absolute certainty as the threaded shank system.

6. ER collet chuck with Morse taper mount

While a number of plain collets meet this requirement, the ER range is now by far the most prominent, although these collets are not intended solely for holding cutters. Because of this, they are considered in detail in Chapter 11 in terms of their use on the lathe.

When using an ER chuck (see **Photo 6**) to hold a cutter, it is essential that it is fully tightened or else the cutter will gradually work out of the collet as it is traversed along the workpiece, causing the cut to deepen. Anyone who has attempted to use a drill chuck will almost certainly have experienced this situation.

Other forms of collet (Morse or R8) fit directly into the machine's taper and use the draw bar to pull the collet into this, enabling it to grip the cutter's shank. These, like the ER collets, may allow the cutter to be withdrawn if not fully tightened. However, they do have an advantage: as the cutter is held much closer to the machine's taper, the set-up is more rigid than using a chuck that projects. This may allow a heavier cut to be taken, and possibly more important a better finish may result. They also create a greater maximum cutter-to-table dimension, which, on rare occasions, may be beneficial, especially on smaller machines.

7. A boring head with number 2 and 3 Morse taper mounts

Having described the types available, my advice would be to obtain a milling cutter chuck made specifically for threaded shank cutters, as this will eliminate any possibility of the cutter being withdrawn from the collet as machining progresses.

Boring head

For want of a better place, I am including this device in this section on cutter holders. The major difference between this and other tool holders is that the position of the cutter within the holder is adjustable. This enables it to bore holes over a range of diameters and, by adjusting the tool between passes, the diameter of the hole can be gradually increased until the required size is achieved.

The head has a fine feed with a calibrated dial for precise setting. This has a limited range, but the tool can be fitted in a number of positions to suit the diameter to be bored. **Photo 7** shows a typical version, a nice feature of which is that it is supplied with both number 2 and number 3 Morse tapers. As a result, it is suitable for both my milling machine and my lathe.

Boring heads are far from essential in the majority of workshops, so it is best to see how

the workshop's range of activities develops before making a purchase. Should one become necessary, the choice is not difficult because there is very little difference between the versions available.

Minor accessories

An essential requirement is a range of relatively simple items that can be used to hold either the workpiece or a device for holding the workpiece firmly onto the table. These include T-nuts, studs, washers, nuts, screws and clamps.

The first option is a clamping kit (**Photo 8**). If possible, do inspect this before purchase because I feel that many are much too bulky for the work likely to be carried out. In the kit shown in the photograph, which is the size intended for my medium-size mill/drill, the stud size is M12, which is far too bulky for virtually all the work that I carry out on it. This problem cannot be avoided by purchasing components individually because there is a standard thread size linked to the T-slot size. Personally, I prefer to make my own clamping components (nuts and screws excluded), as this enables me to

8. The parts from a commercially available clamping kit may be too bulky for most workshop owners' needs.

9. Shop-made light-duty clamping components are preferable to commercially available kits in most cases.

10. A jacking screw is an ideal alternative to fixed height packing because it permits the packing height to be precisely set.

tailor them to their likely use. In this case, I use predominantly M8, with M10 for the occasional heavy-duty application.

Purchasing studs is worthwhile because they will be high tensile and have a short thread at one end to enter the T-nut and a longer thread at the working end. Even here, there is a limited range of lengths, and shortening longer ones to obtain intermediate lengths will almost certainly be necessary.

Photo 9 shows a range of my own shop-made clamping items – and what better for a first project than making a selection of clamping gear. You will first have to make a couple of T-nuts by hand (saw and file) and some simple clamp bars to get you started as, invariably, these will not be supplied with your new machine.

Fixing a workpiece securely to the table is a varied task and a crucial one, because the part may move while being machined if this is not done properly. Unfortunately, the wide variety of shapes and sizes of items that need to be held means this is far too broad a subject o be covered here in detail. Readers should therefore seek other sources of information. The following are the major requirements.

1. Always use enough clamps; too many is far better than too few.
2. If you unable to position all of the ideal number of clamps, consider adding clamps at table level that restrain the edge of the component rather than clamp it.
3. Where possible, the stud should be nearer the workpiece than the packing in order to maximise the clamping force.
4. The packing should be a little higher than the component. My preference is to use a jacking screw because this gives precise control over the height (see Photo 10).
5. When using screws to clamp a vice or other item, make sure that its length does not allow it to bottom in the T-slot. If this happens, you may think that the item is clamped when it is not. As a result, the item being clamped may move when machining commences, with potentially disastrous results.
5. When tightening a nut onto a slotted clamp, use a substantial washer at least 3mm thick. Standard washers will certainly not do!

In addition to bar-type clamps, other clamps may find a use, typically low profile clamps. These clamps are particularly useful when the

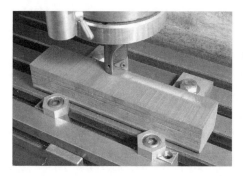

11. Low-profile clamps can be very useful for some applications, typically, where the top surface has to be machined fully.

12. Providing the front edge of a machine vice is parallel to the vice's jaw, using a square off the table's edge to position it is an easy operation.

top surface is to be machined completely (see Photo 11).

Machine vice

Readers may be surprised when I say that, in my estimation, the machine vice is far from essential for the vast majority of tasks undertaken on the milling machine. I attribute its popularity to its apparent ease of use, which leads to it being used when other methods would better meet the requirements. The first problem is accurately positioning the vice on the table, because few vices give any reference point other than the jaws themselves. To do this necessitates setting up a dial test indicator and traversing the slide to check that the jaws are at right angles to, and parallel with, the X-axis and Y-axis. My way around this situation, where the vice construction permits, is to machine the front edge of the base precisely parallel to the jaws. Then all that is required is to use a square off the front edge of the table (see **Photo 12**); this is sufficiently accurate for all but the most demanding situation.

Some vices have locating keys in the base that engage with the T-slots in the machine's table in order to position the vice. This certainly makes positioning the vice a quick and easy operation, but I doubt whether it is sufficiently accurate for some applications. Where precision is important, the keys will have to be removed.

Once the vice is in place, it is still frequently a problem to position the workpiece within the vice, particularly when identical parts are being made. In this case, an angle plate fitted with a guide fence, or two, is far superior.

Despite these reservations, I must admit that I would not run my workshop without a vice for the milling machine. The problem is: which to choose? The essential requirements, in order of priority, are: compatibility in terms of size with the machine on which it is to be used, lack of jaw lift, accuracy and robustness. Choosing a vice for your milling machine may well be one of the most difficult choices you have to make in terms of equipping the workshop. This is because, while there is a vast number to choose from, there is, as I see it, a huge gap in what is available to suit the average size mill/drill or smaller.

Considerations
Jaw lift, if present, occurs when a component is

held towards the top of the jaw, as shown in **Sk. 1**. In a good vice, this is overcome largely by fitting a longer than normal moving jaw and by ensuring all the relevant parts are closely fitting. The length of the keep plate below the jaw is also important.

Accuracy is largely self-explanatory but the main requirements are that the jaws must be at right angles to the base of the vice, and the face on which the jaw slides must be parallel with it. This is because it is these two surfaces that most often position the component for machining.

Robustness is a more debatable requirement because it will depend on the workshop's intended purpose. For example, model engineering in the smaller scales is a quite different situation from making traction engines in the larger sizes.

Size may be the most difficult decision as, in my opinion, most milling machine vice designs are based on vices used on horizontal milling machines, where the load placed on them is far greater than when using a vertical mill. In addition, as the majority of horizontal milling machines have been much larger than the average mill/drill, most of the vices available are too large for most workshops. As an example, a vice with a jaw width of 100mm on a 200mm wide machine table may sound like a suitable combination but, as **Photo 13** shows, this is

13. Choosing the correct size of vice is an essential but not easy task. In this case, the smaller vice has a slightly larger capacity, width and length.

not so. In this case, the vice also has a central fixing at either end but, as the table has four T-slots, it has to be mounted either in front of, or behind centre, and the latter restricts the travel in rearward directions because the base fouls the machine's column.

In most cases, 100mm wide is the smallest size of milling machine vice available, although, in a limited number of cases, 50mm and 75mm sizes are also made. In my estimation, 50mm is far too small for most workshops, but seeing by how much, physically, the 100mm vice is too large, the 75mm vice will probably also be too large, although to a lesser extent, of course.

Another consideration, even if you have a large milling machine, is whether to purchase a vice with a swivelling and/or tilting mechanism as, unless you are likely to make considerable use of this feature, the problem of setting it for normal use outweighs its benefit. Being higher, it will also reduce the available space between workpiece and cutter. Admittedly, the vice itself can usually be removed from the swivelling mechanisms, enabling it to be mounted directly onto the machine's table, but even if this is done, the one shown in Photo 13 is still too wide for the machine table.

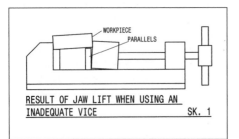

RESULT OF JAW LIFT WHEN USING AN
INADEQUATE VICE   SK. 1

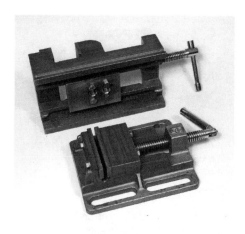

15. Most milling vices are too large for the average and smaller mill/drill, but a toolmaker's vice can be a viable alternative.

14. Here, the smaller of the two vices shown in Photo 13 has been fitted with a longer keep plate to prevent jaw lift. The economy vice (front) has been fitted with a longer jaw and keep plate for the same reason.

However, do **not** use an economy drilling vice unless, like me, you are prepared to do some work on it to make it suitable. **Photo 14** shows two vices that I have modified by lightly skimming all the important surfaces to improve accuracy and to fit a longer jaw and/or jaw keep plate. For medium-duty applications, these are more than adequate. The smaller one may look rather flimsy but do note that, with four fixings, it inherits considerable strength from the table on which it is mounted. The larger one has been modified so that it has similar features to those of a toolmaker's vice. The larger vice is also shown on the left of Photo 13 and actually has a slightly larger capacity – both width and length – than the larger vice in the same photograph.

If you have a medium-size mill/drill, or smaller, the choice is not that simple. As mentioned above, there are a few, like the one shown in Photo 18 , with a jaw width of 75mm that may be worth considering, although some can be very expensive. Failing that, my choice would be one of the larger toolmaker's vices (**Photo 15**). See also Photo 2 which just shows (bottom left hand corner) how this type of vice is anchored to the machine table. If your anticipated milling work falls into the light-duty category, there are a few better-quality drilling vices that may fill the bill (see Chapter 12, Photo 7). Even in this case, fitting a longer keep plate, which is a simple task, is be a good idea and, for best effect, the extension should be in front of the jaw.

Angle plates
These come in two types: fixed angle (90°) and adjustable. The adjustable ones are rather specialised, and most workshops will function adequately without one. They are definitely items to purchase only when the need becomes apparent.

However, fixed-angle angle plates are essential, even more so than a vice in my opinion, because they can satisfactorily hold almost anything that a vice can hold. In addition, they often have two advantages: easier positioning of the workpiece and greater accuracy, which is a major benefit when making batches of components. **Photo**

17. The three common forms of angle plate: a small angle with strengthening webs (left),larger without webs (centre), and without slots (right).

16. It is often easier to position a workpiece using an angle plate rather than a vice.

16 shows a simple example in which a fence has been used to position the component at an angle; if an end stop had also been fitted, it would enable repeat parts to be made to the same length. This would not be easy using a vice, even for a single workpiece.

Once you have decided to obtain an angle plate, there are three options from which to choose (see **Photo 17**).

First, the angle plate can either be a simple right angle or have webs between the two sides for added strength. In this case, I would recommend the angle plate without webs, because these can sometimes be an inconvenience and the added rigidity is seldom of any benefit.

Angle plates are also sold without slots, which may be useful where a complex workpiece demands fixings in places that slots would not provide. In this case, the angle plate can be drilled for fixings specifically for the job in hand and is especially suitable for making jigs for batch production. However, for general-purpose

work the slotted plate is to be preferred.

Size is another consideration and, for the average mill/drill, a main face size of around 150mm wide by 100mm high is probably a good size.

Another advantage of the angle plate is that, if held in the bench vice with the working face horizontal, it will often be easier to position and fix the workpiece. The complete assembly can then be taken to the machine table for the required machining to be carried out.

Parallels

Parallels, which are used to pack up the workpiece, either in the vice, when the height of the workpiece is less than the jaws, or against the angle plate (as shown in **Photo 18**), are an essential requirement for the milling machine. Less essential, but still useful, are 1-2-3 blocks. A typical example of their use is shown in **Photo 19**, where the base of a small machine vice is being machined to ensure it is parallel with the face on which the jaw will eventually slide.

V blocks

These are of limited use on the milling machine for a number of reasons (and, in my workshop, I have adopted a method that I consider far superior). However, if V blocks are available and you are considering a purchase, you should

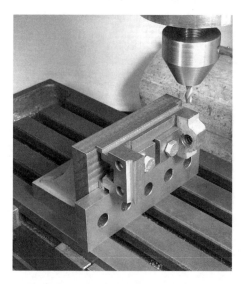

18. Parallels are an essential accessory for use on the milling machine. The one shown here is being used to position a small vice for machining the fixing groove.

take note of the following. During the milling process, the security of the workpiece is vital, but the clamps provided with the block will be inadequate for all but the lightest of duties.

19. Using a 1-2-3 block to support the vice casting (see also Photo 18).

20. The method shown on the left has many advantages over using a conventional V block (right).

Even if you consider them adequate for the task in hand, the V block also needs securing to the table, which does not leave a lot of room for the V block's own clamps.

As an alternative to the block's own clamps, the clamps that are used generally on the milling machine can be employed for the task, as shown in Photo 20 (right). Even so, this approach has a number of disadvantages:

1. The block itself is loose until the workpiece is clamped and some means of positioning it must be provided. As the photograph shows, the locating plates have been clamped to the machine table for positioning the V block.
2. The system will not work with small diameters unless some packing is placed between the workpiece and the clamp.
3. The clamping force will attempt to spread the block, and it is not unknown for blocks to split into two parts if the clamps are overtightened.

However, all is not lost because the alternative method shown on the left of the photograph has many advantages:

•   It will work with a large range of diameters, say, from 2mm upwards, with the upper limit dictated only by the size of the machine.

- It is easy to set up.
- It is very secure.
- Very long items can be easily supported.
- No expensive items are required.

First, fix the first plate on the machine table, using a square off the front edge of the table to position it. Next, take a piece of material about half as wide as the diameter of the workpiece to be supported and use this as a spacer to position the second plate for clamping to the machine table. Add the workpiece and clamp it into place. Large diameters will require thicker plates, and longer workpieces will require longer plates, perhaps with two clamps.

Using a magnetic V block is a possibility if the task is very light, but some means of accurately placing the block on the table will still be necessary (see Photo 21). Note that, even in this case, the magnetic grip is not completely reliable and, as the photograph shows, support plates have been added to the machine table. In addition, an end stop in the form of an angle plate has been fitted to prevent the workpiece sliding along the V block. This is not a procedure to adopt without considerable thought, and it is a case of, if in doubt, don't! A magnetic V block is therefore far from being an essential workshop item.

Positioning devices

Once the workpiece has been accurately positioned in relation to the machine's X- and Y- axes, it may still be necessary to position the cutter accurately relative to the workpiece, typically an edge. There are a number of methods of achieving this, ranging from those that cost virtually nothing to others that will need to be purchased. Fortunately, even the most costly are are not too expensive.

21. A magnetic V block should only be used for light duties and then only when security of the workpiece and V block is absolutely certain. If in doubt, use another method.

One method is to start the cutter and run it up to the side of the workpiece while listening for the sound of the cutter making contact with the workpiece or looking out for the first signs of the workpiece being machined. In the latter case, covering the surface with marking blue will help. These methods have the disadvantage that the edge of the workpiece will be marked.

The traditional method of overcoming this is to moisten a piece of very thin paper and stick it to the workpiece being tested. Thus, when the cutter comes into contact with the paper, it will drag it from the workpiece. This indicates that the distance between the cutter and the workpiece is nominally equal to the thickness of the paper. Another method that does not deface the workpiece is to place a short piece of round material in the chuck and a feeler gauge between the rod and the workpiece and to traverse the table until the feeler is just trapped. In a more advanced version of this (**Photo 22**), the test piece has a light inside it that comes on the moment it contacts the workpiece.

Once you know the diameter of the item being

22. The light in this edge finder comes on when it contacts the item being located.

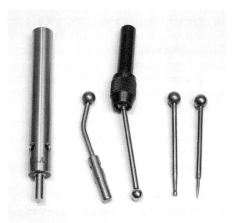

23. Two edge finders: illuminated and a wiggler.

but even the more accurate collet chuck is likely to have some error, especially if it is at a distance from the chuck itself.

A device that attempts to overcome this problem is an edge finder, often referred to as a "wiggler". This is shown in **Photo 23** (right), together with an electrical tester (left). As the photograph shows, there are a number of test pieces but all work in the same way. The holder together with the chosen test piece, are joined in a ball joint that allows the test piece to be set at an angle to the holder. With the workpiece away from the edge finder and the machine running, the end of the test piece will rotate in a circle. If the workpiece is then moved up to the tester, gradually reducing the diameter of the circle, it will eventually reach a point where the end of the tester ceases to scribe a circle but just rotates on its own axis. In this situation, the advantage of the system is that, no matter how inaccurate the chuck holding the device, the end of the tester will be exactly on the machine's spindle axis.

At this point, the spindle's axis is just half

used to locate the edge, be it a cutter, rod or electrical tester, you will then need to traverse the table by half its diameter and the machine spindle's axis will be above the edge being tested. It will then be a case of traversing the table further as the dimensions of the workpiece require.

All the above have one disadvantage: they cannot easily take account of test items not running perfectly true. This is a particular problem if the test item is held in a drill chuck, the diameter of the test piece away from the workpiece's edge. Unfortunately, visual determination of just when the tester ceases to scribe a circle is far from easy. However, this is not considered necessary because, if the workpiece is traversed further, the tester will be pushed off centre and will again attempt to scribe a circle. However, as part of the circle will now be within the workpiece itself, this is impossible and the end of the tester will rapidly run to one side.

Just how much more accurate this is than the other methods will, I suppose, depend on the accuracy of the chucks holding the test pieces. For my part, I would suggest that allowing the cutter to just touch the workpiece or adding thin paper are more than adequate for the vast majority of applications.

Major accessories
A number of major accessories remain to be considered but they should definitely not be purchased until the workshop's activities show a need for them.

Dividing heads
For simple applications, including the occasional gear, a shop-made dividing head (**Photo 24**, left) will be more than adequate. Although the semi-universal dividing head (right) will provide many more divisions, only a universal head will fill in all the gaps up to 380 divisions, although 380 divisions are unlikely to be required in most workshops.

The uses for dividing heads are many and varied, and range from the simple to the very complex. At the simple end of the spectrum is the need to machine a square for mounting an operating handle (**Photo 25**). Beyond this, there is the need for many different gears, for example, when clock-making.

24. Dividing heads: shop-made (left) and commercially available (right).

5C fixtures
Three accessories used for holding round workpieces, all of which use the 5C collet as the means of holding the part, are shown in **Photo 26**.

The first is a simple dividing device (left), normally known as a spin index fixture, which can be set in one-degree increments through a full 360°. This one is particularly interesting because it is supplied with an adapter (left) and

25. The commercial dividing head being used to machine a square for accepting a drive handle

26. Three forms of 5C fixtures: spin index fixture (left); fixture with closing ring (centre); fixture without closing ring (right).

27. Rotary tables: commercially available (left) and shop-made (right).

closing ring (centre left), enabling it also to use ER32 collets, which have a wide holding range. An ER32 collet included (centre rig ht) with a 5C collet (right).

Do not think that the ability to be set in one-degree increments makes this a suitable alternative to a more expensive dividing head. As an example, consider the need to cut a 50-tooth gear. This would require an angle of movement between the teeth of 360/50 (i.e. 7.2°), which is obviously not possible.

The other two fixtures are simple devices for holding components using only 5C collets. These can be mounted either horizontally or vertically for machining, as the part requires. However, there is an interesting difference between the two devices, which was briefly mentioned in the discussion on collets in Chapter 11.

The fixture in the centre of the photograph has a closing ring to push the collet into its internal taper in order to close the collet and, with this arrangement, the amount that the collet enters its internal taper will depend on the workpieces diameter. Typically, with a smaller part, the collet will enter further.

The fixture on the right of the photograph, however, does not include a closing ring. In this case, the collet is screwed into the base of the fixture using the collet's threaded end (as shown), and is closed by the internal taper moving forward. With this arrangement, the front of the collet will remain in the same position no matter what the diameter of the part being machined. This is very important where second operation work requires accurate machining in relation to a flange on the workpiece that is located against the collet's front face.

Rotary tables
Commercially available rotary tables (**Photo 27**, left) can be supplied with added parts to make them suitable for dividing applications (that on the right is a shop-made table). However, these tables are primarily intended for machining curved surfaces or slots, typically as seen in the changewheel quadrant (**Photo 28**). Like the above major items, a rotary table should not be purchased until there is an obvious need for one.

Taking a cut is easy
Once you have acquired the necessary accessories, and are ready to start machining, you may find that the knowledge you require is not what you expected. In my opinion, apart from the sharpening of workshop tooling, the

28. A rotary table is ideal for making the curved slot seen in this changewheel quadrant.

milling machine is more demanding in terms of decision-making than any other machine. This is not due to the complexities of applying the cutter to the workpiece but to mounting the workpiece prior to a cut being taken. This is unlike the lathe, where a wider range of operations is possible, but where practically all of them can be carried out with reference to the book, so to speak. Mounting components ready for machining covers a wide range of situations, many of which will be unique. Therefore, experience with a wide range of tasks, perhaps with some helpful reading, is essential if you are to become at home with using the milling machine. Removing metal is relatively simple!

Chapter 15

Grinders and motorized saws

Grinders

Grinders for use in the home workshop fall into three categories:

1. off-hand grinders – essential
2. tool and cutter grinders – nice to have, but there are other ways
3. a surface grinder – an absolute luxury!

Off-hand grinders

In almost all home workshops, the off-hand grinder (**Photo 1**) will be the only grinding facility available. This is unfortunate because the task that it is likely to be called upon to undertake, namely the sharpening of workshop cutters, will be the most ineffective operation carried out in the workshop.

The alternative is a tool and cutter grinder (see below). For readers who wish to take the off-hand grinder route there are three possibilities:

1. to make your own machine, for example, the Quorn
2. to purchase a machine aimed at the small workshop (**Photo 2**).
3. to purchase a secondhand industrial machine

1. A typical off-hand grinder. Unfortunately, this is often the only sharpening facility available in the small workshop.

For most workshop owners, the first will be too large a task, the second will be too expensive and the third will involve too large a machine. Because of this, most people will understandably attempt to make do with the off-hand grinder as purchased.

A few workshop owners may be able to produce good results for items such as lathe tools purely free hand but, for many, even with these, the results will be less than acceptable. One area that often raises controversy is the sharpening

2. The universal cutter grinder (Warco).

3. Except for woodworking tools, drill-grinding fixtures are the only sharpening accessory commercially available for use with an off-hand grinder.

of drills unaided, which some people claim to be able to accomplish. I am sure that, with plenty of practice, some workshop owners are able to produce a working drill; for others, the number of drills that require sharpening will not provide them with sufficient experience to perfect the process. This still leaves cutting tools, such as end mills and slot drills, which are totally impossible to sharpen free hand.

Two requirements need to be met when sharpening a drill:

1.   it should cut freely
2.   it should cut to size.

Although the first is relatively easy to achieve, the latter cannot be guaranteed. It is probably the ability to cut freely that prompts some people to claim that they have mastered the art, but there is no point in having a set of drills in 0.1mm increments if the 8.3mm drill cuts an 8.4mm diameter hole, or maybe larger.

Therefore, for most workshop owners, a drill-grinding jig (**Photo 3**) is an essential item. Although it needs to be set up carefully, once you understand the requirements, it will produce good results with ease and is not expensive.

Unfortunately, except for a few woodworking tools, the drill-sharpening jig is the only off-hand grinder accessory available for a specific task. Consequently, you will be faced with grinding the rest of your cutters free hand, which ranges from just possible for most lathe tools to impossible for most milling cutters. You can get round this situation by making a relatively simply rest (such as that in **Photo 4**) and a few equally simple accessories (**Photo 5**), which will meet practically all your sharpening requirements. Only the end-mill sharpening accessory (**Photo 6**) borders on the complex, but even this should be within the range of most workshop owner's capabilities.

Details for making the rest and its accessories can be found in the book *Tool and Cutter Sharpening* (Workshop Practice Series Number 38.).

4. To gain the best from your off-hand grinder, you will need to make a rest with a controlled feed.

5. The rest shown in Photo 4 will still need some simple accessories if its benefits are to be realised.

6. An end-mill sharpening fixture for use with the grinding rest shown in Photo 4.

Apart from the improved rest, only one other item is necessary: a wheel dresser. The effectiveness of a wheel's surface is reduced with use and, in order to restore its full working condition, it has to be broken away by applying a wheel dresser. Two versions of wheel dresser are shown in **Photo 7**: one with a single diamond (left) and one with multiple, but much smaller, diamonds (right). Both work well, but I would opt for the multiple diamond dresser. Another form of wheel dresser has star-shaped wheels but I consider this more appropriate to wheels larger than those used in the home workshop.

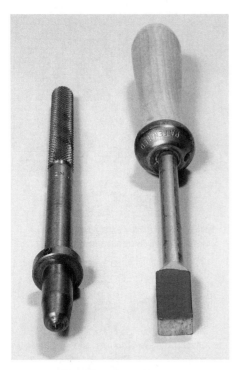

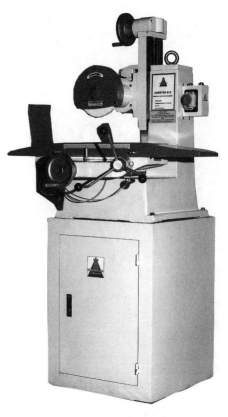

7. Two versions of wheel dresser: single diamond (left), multiple diamond (right).

Tool and cutter grinder

If the above approach does not appeal, the only option is to obtain a small tool and cutter grinder or a larger secondhand industrial version.

***

Whatever method you adopt, the sharpening of workshop tools requires much care in setting up and, as a result, is not a task that can be completed quickly, whatever your equipment.

If you opt for an off-hand grinder, there are many makes to choose from and, because they show little variation, any of them should be suitable. The only decision is size and, in

8. A surface grinder is a luxury for almost all workshops (Chester).

this respect, I would recommend a wheel size of 150mm. However, please do not adopt the totally free-hand approach because working with less than perfectly sharpened tools will frequently lead to a drop in satisfaction with the work being undertaken.

Surface grinder

The surface grinder (Photo 8) is rarely found in the home workshop, but is included for the sake of completeness. These grinders are used to remove very small amounts of metal, whilst at the same time producing an accurately flat surface. They also produce the bright but very slightly frosted surface finish present on many commercial tools, such as vices, angle plates, etc.

Typical of a simple application is the creation of the working surface of a small surface plate, the grinder shown in the photograph being able to cover a surface of 300mm × 150mm. A more demanding task is machining out any distortion resulting from hardening an item, typically a toolmaker's vice, although such requirements will rarely occur in the home workshop. Whilst many workshop owners would be delighted to own one of these grinders in order to achieve a professional-looking finish, most will accept that the machining lines left by the end mill will have to stay.

Belt and disk sanders

If you would like to be able to take out machining marks or remove damage marks, or maybe rust, there is still another option, although it lacks the accuracy of the surface grinder. This is to use a belt or disk sander, as shown in **Photo 9**. However, these types of sander need to be used with care because they can remove metal at a greater rate than most people would expect.

Consider having machined on the milling machine the toolmaker's vice, in the last chapter (Chapter 14, Photo 15) and with its sides both square and parallel to one another. Applying the surfaces to the belt to achieve a bright finish could easily destroy the accuracy achieved.

Whether or not you equip your workshop with one of these sanders depends on the calibre of the work that you wish to undertake; for example, if it includes producing a lot of small welded assemblies then having one to dress the welds would almost certainly be worthwhile.

9. A belt and disk sander is useful for cleaning up welds and damaged surfaces, as well as removing machining marks (Chester).

Motorised saws

Motorised saws fall into two main types: those with a horizontal action and those with a vertical action. Horizontal machines are designed primarily for cutting lengths from metal bars. On the other hand, vertical saws, although they can be used for this task, are designed primarily for making longer cuts in thinner materials, either straight or curved. One major difference is that the horizontal saw can be left to complete a cut whilst the vertical machine has to be hand fed.

The use of a motorised saw will save you a lot of hard work and, unless you are skilled in the process, will produce more accurate results. Even more important, where a considerable amount of sawing is required, it may turn an impracticable job into one that can be attempted with ease.

What are your options if you decide that you need a motorised saw? Disregarding others, such as cut-off saws with a rotating disk, there are really only two types suitable for the home workshop:

1. a hack saw with a reciprocating action
2. a horizontal band saw, in which the band runs continuously in one direction.

Hack saw

Although hack-saw blades are cheaper than band-saw blades, you will probably use more of them so the cost may not be very different. The major advantage of the hack saw is that blades can be changed much more easily and, as a result, you are more likely to change to a different pitch blade when circumstances dictate. This is certainly not the case when using a band saw. Motorised hack saws have been largely replaced by horizontal band saws so there is now much less choice.

Horizontal band saw

The major advantage of the horizontal band saw is that it cuts continuously, and thus completes the task more rapidly than other similar-size machines.

Photo 10 shows a horizontal band saw typical of those available for use in the home workshop. This can cut bar up to 110mm diameter and rectangular bar 150mm wide and is typical of all machines of this type. The vice jaws can be pivoted up to 45°, allowing angled cuts to be made, although this reduces the size of bar that can be cut

One of the major disadvantages of these saws is that they take up a large amount of floor space, which is a major consideration for those with a

10. A horizontal band saw will minimise a lot of hard graft cutting bar materials.

small workshop. Similar, and smaller, machines are available for bench mounting, although they are still quite large. This is where the powered hack saws, which are small enough for bench mounting, score. However, both the small horizontal machine (**Photo 11**) and the hack saw (**Photo 12**) are relatively heavy, the hack saw particularly so at 68 kg. For most people, these will machines that require a permanent home, rather than being moved into place when required for use, and available bench space may be a major consideration.

As a spot or two of rust will not seriously affect the horizontal band saw, you may be prepared to keep it in the garage, along with the car. This machine will finish most tasks in a minute or two, so you will not have to spend much time in a cold garage.

144

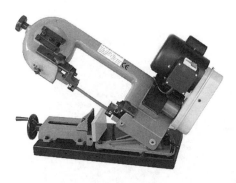

11. A small bench-mounted horizontal band saw may not require any floor space but could take up valuable bench space (Warco).

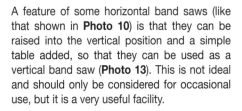

12. A bench-mounted hack saw is an alternative to the horizontal band saw but heavy if you wish to store it away from the bench top when not in use (Arc Euro trade).

13. Some horizontal machines can be used in a vertical mode but this facility should only be considered acceptable for occasional use.

14. Where there is a frequent need for a vertical machine, one like this should be considered.

A feature of some horizontal band saws (like that shown in **Photo 10**) is that they can be raised into the vertical position and a simple table added, so that they can be used as a vertical band saw (**Photo 13**). This is not ideal and should only be considered for occasional use, but it is a very useful facility.

However, if you are likely to have a frequent requirement for a vertical saw, you should consider obtaining a bench- or floor-mounted saw (see **Photo 14**).

15. *If your interest requires shaping thin materials, a motorised fret saw would be worth considering.*

Fret saw

One other type of saw that is likely to be of use in the home workshop is the fret saw. This will be of considerable help if your workshop activities require the shaping of thin metal components, such as the side frames of a clock. The saw illustrated in **Photo 15** is typical of those used for carrying out such tasks.

Chapter 16

Presses, sheet metal machines, welders and shapers

These four items are less likely to be found in most home workshops but nonetheless some people find them very useful.

Presses

Except perhaps for a shaping machine and surface grinder, a press is probably the least likely major machine to be found in the average home workshop. So do you need one?

Uses

The extent to which a press will be needed depends on the workshop's activity, but all workshop owners will probably find one useful for the occasional task. In many cases, these tasks would be much more difficult if attempted by any other means. An important feature of using a press is that, once it is set up, a task can be performed in a matter of seconds. It is therefore highly efficient when it comes to making batches of components.

Bending

Probably top of the list of possible uses is the bending of strip and sheet materials, which is a task that it can do with ease, providing the item is being made of bending quality material.

1. By repeat punching at about 1/4 of the hole's diameter, slots can easily be produced (right of picture) using a fly press.

Punching holes

Another common use of a press is to punch holes. This is a particularly useful alternative when drilling large holes in thin sheet, for example, a 15mm diameter hole into a 0.5mm thick workpiece, which is far from easy.

Another advantage of using the press to punch holes is that part holes can be made, thus enabling slots to be made by repeated

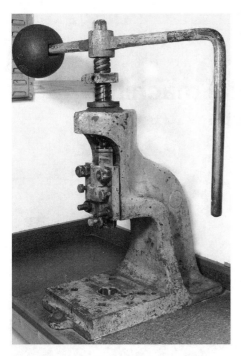

2. A much-used small fly press, 3 tons nominal size.

parts to length can be carried out on other materials, not just metal, typically, card, leather and plastic.

Force fitting and removing.
Whilst a vice can be used for force fitting one part into another, this is often not possible if the component is large. For this operation, a press is an ideal tool.

Types of press
In industry, presses will often be large and powered, but those in the home workshop will always be small and hand operated.

Fly presses
These are made in a range of sizes, the one shown in **Photo 2** being one of the smaller ones, with a throat depth of 120mm and a height of 200mm. This is a much used, perhaps even abused, version of this form of press that was salvaged from an industrial background.

operations at, say, 1/4 of the hole's diameter. To make sure the slot is straight, a fence needs to be set up so that the workpiece can be slid against it. Photo 1 shows an example of this, but unfortunately, the guide fence is hidden under the stripper plate. This principle can be extended to make large rectangular and round holes.

Cropping
If the batch production of parts made from strip material is necessary, it might be worthwhile equipping the press with a mini guillotine for cropping parts to length. With an end stop set, making a batch of parts all the same length will be very time-efficient.

Bear in mind that punching holes and cropping

In terms of the pressure provided (tonnage), it can be seen from the photograph that the ram is operated via a coarse thread rotated by means of a handle. In use, the handle is rotated quickly so that the energy stored in the ball, seen on the end of the arm, provides the power required when the punch contacts the workpiece. Herein lies the scope for abuse as the pressure available will depend on the rate at which the handle is let fly (hence the name of the press?). This particular press has a nominal rating of 3 tons, giving it the ability, for example, to punch a 15mm hole through 1.5mm thick steel sheet.

The coarse thread that operates the ram is a square thread but its outer diameter also has a fine thread on which an adjustable down-feed stop is provided (**Photo 3**). This can be set to ensure the punch only just enters the die, or when carrying out bending operations, to set

3. A fine pitch thread is provided on the outer diameter to provide the fine adjustment for a down-feed stop.

4. A 1/2 ton arbor press.

the angle of the bend being made. Fly presses are very robust machines and even one that has been much neglected, like the one in the previous photograph, should be more than adequate for home workshop use.

Arbor presses

Primarily intended for assembly work, arbor presses (**Photo 4**) are typically used for light-duty riveting, press fitting one part into another, etc. They are made in a range of sizes, commonly sizes 0 to size 3, but larger sizes are also available. Their nominal tonnage ratings are 0.5, 1, 2 and 3 tons. However, some tests carried out on the one in the photograph (size 0, 0.5 tons) showed that, with a larger diameter and longer handle fitted, 1 ton was achievable

and without noticeable stress to the press. Arbor presses are widely available and, at the smaller sizes, economically priced.

Although designed for assembly duties, with a little attention, they can carry out much that a fly press can, albeit at a much lighter load. The most likely problem will be the fit of the ram. Readers will, I am sure, appreciate that, when punching holes, the clearance between the punch and the die will be quite small and any clearance between the ram and the press body will allow the end of the punch to wander, so that the punch and die may foul each other, causing premature wear.

The press in the photograph originally only had

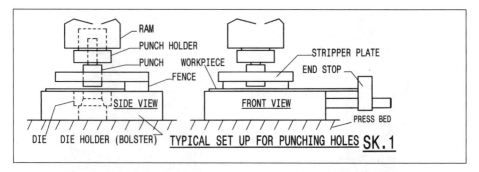

RAM
PUNCH HOLDER
PUNCH WORKPIECE
FENCE
STRIPPER PLATE
END STOP
SIDE VIEW
FRONT VIEW
PRESS BED
DIE DIE HOLDER (BOLSTER) TYPICAL SET UP FOR PUNCHING HOLES SK.1

a gib strip on the front face of the ram, allowing the end of the punch to move from left to right. A second gib strip had to be added, as the four screws in the photograph make evident. This is a simple improvement but some arbor presses already fitted with two gibs are now being advertised.

Hydraulic presses
I mention these only for completeness because their uses are very limited: pressing a shaft, into or out of a gear for example. However, they are commonly available and can easily achieve a greater tonnage than the other presses mentioned. Their construction does not lend itself to fitting accessories for punching holes, although I think bending workpieces would be achievable.

Accessories
As with other machines, the press is capable of very little without some additional items. Consider the task of punching holes, where a punch and die of the required size will be necessary. Unfortunately, what first appears to be an easy operation is not without problems. Top of the list is that, once the hole has been punched, the punch will be firmly gripped by the workpiece and some method of extricating it must be provided. In order to do this, a stripper plate, like the one in **Sk. 1**, is necessary.

Other provisions in this set-up are a locating

fence and an end stop to control the position of the hole relative to the workpiece's edge and end. In addition, holders are provided to limit the physical size of each punch and die, rather than fitting the punches directly into the ram and the die onto the press bed. The holder for the die is often called a bolster.

When working with thin material, holes often need to be made in relatively large sheets. Because of this, the stripper plate illustrated in **Sk. 1** becomes impracticable so a stripper mounted off the upper framework of the press is used. **Photo 5** shows an example that also

5. An overhead stripper assembly makes it possible to punch holes in large sheets. The set-up also includes an auxiliary table for supporting larger workpieces.

6. A set of typical parts for use on a fly press when punching holes.

7. Accessories for an arbor press for use when punching holes.

includes an added support plate for larger workpieces.

Photo 6 shows a range of items that are needed to provide these facilities on the fly press whilst **Photo 7** shows a similar range of equipment, but smaller, for use on the arbor press. Most of the items shown for use on the fly press are available commercially but the smaller assembly for use on the arbor press will have to be shop made.

Punches and dies
A punch and die for every size of hole might appear to be an expensive requirement. Fortunately, punches and dies do not have to be made from hardened steel, normal mild steel being more than adequate for anything other than mass production. More than 100 holes

plus can easily be made with unhardened mild steel punches and dies and, when they are blunt and producing poor holes, the ends can easily be faced on the lathe and given a new lease of life. However, there could be a problem with non-hard punches and dies because, if they are used to punch a small hole in a relatively thick workpiece, say 4mm diameter into 3mm thick, the punch may collapse.

Another advantage is that soft punches and dies made for a one-off job can later be re-machined for other diameters. With rather more care, shapes other than round can also be made.

An additional complication is that, in theory, the clearance between punch and die is dependent on the thickness of the material being punched, the difference in their diameters being approximately equal to 0.1 times the material thickness. However, in general, this value is not critical.

To limit the number of blanks held in the die, and thus minimise the force required to push them through, the rear should either be tapered (**Sk. 2A**) or opened up with a slightly larger drill (**Sk. 2B**).

An arbor press set up for punching holes is

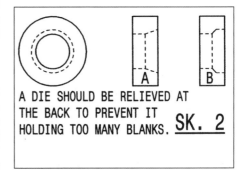

A DIE SHOULD BE RELIEVED AT THE BACK TO PREVENT IT HOLDING TOO MANY BLANKS. SK. 2

8. *An arbor press set up for punching holes. Note the workpiece on the right.*

shown in **Photo 8**. (A similar set-up on a fly press was shown in Photo 1.)

Bending

Using a press for bending either strip or plate is easier than punching holes because it requires simpler equipment. Typically, **Sk. 3** shows how a V form punch and die can be used to create a bend. Unfortunately, although the equipment is simple, the process is not without its complications. Most importantly, when the punch is raised, the angle will spring back a little, so if the angle of both the punch and die is 90°, the resulting bend will be a few degrees less.

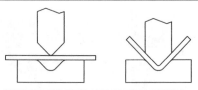

SPRING BACK AFTER BENDING MAKES THIS METHOD UNSUITABLE FOR SMALL QUANTITIES AS BOTH THE PUNCH AND DIE REQUIRE TO BE LESS THAN 90° AND BY AN AMOUNT DEPENDANT ON THE MATERIAL BEING BENT AND ITS THICKNESS. SK. 3

Reducing the angle of the punch alone will help, but the extent to which this is done can only be determined by trial and error. As a result, an alternative approach must be adopted, at least in the home workshop. In any case, machining an internal V with an angle of less than 90° is not straightforward.

Sk. 4 shows a simpler method that will enable the operator to compensate for variations mentioned above by varying the amount by which the punch enters the die. This, I believe, is called "air bending", for obvious reasons, and it is perfectly adequate for the small-quantity work likely to surface in the home workshop. **Photo 9** shows an example of this method and, as close examination will show, neither the punch nor the die is machined with a V formation.

Photo 10 shows some typical equipment used for bending on the fly press, on which it can be seen that the wide die is equipped with a fence for setting the position of the bend relative to the part's edge. (This can also be seen in Photo 9).

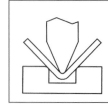

WITH THIS METHOD SPRING BACK WITH VARYING METALS CAN BE OVERCOME BY ADJUSTING THE AMOUNT THAT THE PUNCH ENTERS THE DIE.

SK. 4

9. Using a fly press for bending sheet steel.

10. Accessories to enable bending of sheet and strip materials using a fly press.

11. Bending strip material on the fly press.

The narrower punch and die also shown illustrates a vital requirement, namely that thicker materials will require a wider die and a larger radius on the punch. **Photo 11** shows these being used and also illustrates that, for a one-off bend, or just a few, there is no need to fix the die. It also shows that the die has been made with a V of much less than 90°.

Note that the more common strip-steel specifications are not ideal for bending unless they are annealed, so bending quality steel is a better option.

Installation

Installing a fly press in the workshop calls for a very robust bench, which must itself be firmly anchored to the workshop floor and/or wall. In addition, there must be enough space for the handle to be rotated fully through 360°. As a result, even a small fly press will take up much more space than the area of its base would suggest. Even so, the bench space on either side of it can be used for other things when the press is not in use, or even left there providing they do not restrict the handle's movement. While an arbor press requires much less space and is not quite so demanding with regard to the rigidity of its mounting, it still needs to be very secure.

153

Need for?

Whilst I feel that every workshop owner would find a use for a fly press at some time, this may not be sufficient to justify the space that it requires. Think carefully about the situation before deciding to work without one.

Sheet metal machines

In an industrial workshop, guillotines and press brakes (bending machines) enable a speed and quality of work to be achieved that has hitherto been almost impossible in the home workshop. This is quite different from the situation with lathes and milling machines, where what is done in the home workshop compares favourably with similar processes in the industrial world. However, the "3-in-1 universal sheet metal machines" (**Photo 12**) that have become available in recent years have gone some way to narrowing the gap, albeit at a much smaller size. These machines contain three devices – a guillotine, press brake and three-roll bender – and are available in widths of between 300mm and 1000mm.

Suppliers' specifications for these machines give figures for shearing sheet steel of between 0.6mm and 1mm for what appears to be essentially the same machine. Therefore, if your requirement is to shear thicker material, discuss this in detail with the supplier to be sure that this can be done without the machine complaining. However, if your requirement is within the machine's range, it is certainly worth considering because the alternative methods of cutting and bending sheet materials are far less satisfactory. With softer materials, such as aluminium, thicker material could be sheared, say 1.5mm, by a machine quoted as suitable for 1mm when cutting steel.

The quoted figures for bending also vary; sometimes they are the same as the shearing

12. 3-in-1 sheet metal machines are available in a range of widths (Warco).

capability and sometimes rather more. Personally, I think that they could bend thicker material than they could shear, especially if making a bend of less than the full width of the machine. In this respect 1.5mm on a machine quoted as shearing 1mm would seem very likely, although you should check with the supplier.

The upper bending V is supplied in sections of varying widths, enabling them to be set up in suitable widths for bending boxes.

The upper part of the machine is a three-roll bender. This will enable sheets or thin bar materials that have become slightly curved in storage to be straightened. More importantly, as there is no real alternative, they can be used to produce curved items and cylinders from sheet materials and thin strip.

As an alternative to the above, **Photo 13** shows four items for cutting sheet metal: a jig saw, nibbler and Pencut attachments for use with a power drill, and a small guillotine. In my opinion, the jig saw is the one to choose because it can be used to cut a wide range of

13. Four methods of cutting sheet materials: a jig saw, Pencut and nibbler attachments for using with a power tool, and a small guillotine.

materials and much thicker softer materials, such as plastic and timber. It can also follow curves. With a reasonably powerful saw, it should even be possible to cut steel of 3mm thickness, although on the downside, it will be slow and difficult to keep a straight line.

The nibbler and Pencut power tool attachments will be limited to a thickness of around 1mm, whilst the small guillotine will have limited use as it is only suitable for very thin materials (0.5mm maximum I would suggest). Much larger versions are available, but they tend to bend the material.

There are alternative methods for bending, other than those available in the 3-in-1 machine, but they either have a similar capacity or, if capable of bending thicker materials, are much larger and/or expensive. If you can limit the width to around 200mm, a fly press would be worth considering. However, if you need a more substantial bender, arm yourself with a range of catalogues so that you can compare what is available.

Welding
Welding is quite unlike most other activities in the workshop in that it is skill, rather than knowledge, that has to be acquired. Despite considering that I know all the essentials, I still find welding very difficult to master. In my defence, my infrequent use of the process has not helped, and I suspect many other workshop owners are in the same situation. This is without doubt a case where practice makes perfect.

Electric welding equipment
There are two main types of electric welders but both work on the same basic principle, i.e. an electric current passes from the welding torch into the workpiece creating an arc that melts both halves of the item being welded. In addition, extra metal is deposited by the torch to further improve the bond. In other respects, there are some major differences.

Arc welders
For many years, arc welders were the only welding tool available. They are still worth considering if the initial cost of the equipment needs to be kept down, especially if their eventual usage is likely to be low.

To establish the arc, they use flux-coated welding rods, which will need replacing as each rod burns down to its end. Typically, each rod will weld a few metres of weld.

MIG welders (metal inert gas)
In these welders, the rod is replaced by a roll of fine wire that is fed through a pipe to the torch, thus avoiding the need for frequent stops to replace the rods. Also fed down the pipe is a gas that surrounds the weld as it is being made, preventing oxidization taking place. This process may be considered easier than arc welding, but I am still some way from mastering the process. MIG welding is also preferable to arc welding when welding thin sheets. This makes it a good choice for carrying out repairs to car bodywork.

Safety equipment

In addition to the welder itself, a number of safety items will be required. An absolutely essential item is a face mask with a suitably darkened glass visor. The type of visor that starts clear but darkens instantaneously as soon as the arc is struck makes the process somewhat easier. Also essential are some leather gauntlets and either a leather apron or, failing that , some heavy-duty overalls that will not catch fire if the occasion spark lands on them.

***

If you feel that welding will be a frequent requirement, or one where second best will not do, try to find a local technical college which runs a welding course that you can attend. Failing that, get some advice from a knowledgeable exponent of the art - and I do believe it is an art - or, at the very least, read a good book on the subject and collect a large pile of scrap metal on which to practise.

14. A model of an early belt-driven shaping machine, a good starter project for the workshop owner who has not yet decided the workshop's use.

Shapers

These machines were once much more common than the milling machine but, today, they are almost non-existent in the home workshop. During the first half of the twentieth century, a shaper was frequently found in the home workshop but it was invariably a hand-operated machine. This limited the size of the tasks undertaken but no doubt this was largely in keeping with the size of the projects undertaken at the time.

I had anticipated that the shaper had largely disappeared from the industrial scene as well, but a search on the Internet showed that new machines are still being made, although these are very large and completely outside the range appropriate to the home workshop. Because of this, should the reader decide

that a shaper would be a useful acquisition then a secondhand version is the only option. I suspect that even these are becoming less easy to find, although small machines are still advertised occasionally by suppliers of used machines.

Photo 14 shows a typical early belt-driven shaper – and if it doesn't look quite right that is because it is a model rather than a full-size machine. I have included this because it occurs to me that the reader may still be unsure of the direction their workshop is to take and what better than to make the first project a model of an early machine tool such as this! (See Information section for further details.)

For the reader who is not conversant with the shaper's operation, its single-point cutter works with a reciprocating motion, cutting on the forward stroke but raised on its return. At the end of the cycle, the workpiece is moved over slightly and a further cut is taken. Both the length of the stroke and the distance that the workpiece moves between cuts can be set to suit the part being machined.

What then are the advantages of a powered shaper?

1. The tools that they use are the same as those used on the lathe, but they are much easier to maintain than milling cutters. In particular, when machining castings, a simple tungsten carbide tipped tool can be used that is very cheap and easily sharpened when blunt.
2. The surface finish that they produce is far superior to that achieved with a milling machine, especially if the milling cutter is less than sharp. (Sharpening milling cutters is so difficult that it is easy to neglect this task.)
3. Once the length of stroke and width of cut have been set, the shaper can be left to complete the machining of the part's surface of its own accord once a few passes of the tool have been completed to check that all is well. I am not suggesting that the operator does not need be present but the time can be spent on some other minor workshop activity – such as sweeping the floor!

If both the finance and space are available, I believe many workshop owners will find good reasons for owning a shaper, not in place of, but in addition to, a milling machine. I, for one, would certainly have one if I had the space.

Chapter 17

Final Comments

Information

Having reached the end of the book, I would not like readers to think that my workshop faithfully follows all my recommendations, because this is not the case. The book has been written as a result of the lessons I have learnt on the way. Some of these I took note of and carried out the necessary changes; for others, this is just not possible. But I wish that I had made a larger workshop so that there would be space for a shaping machine!

Chapter 7
Harold Hall, *Model Engineers' Workshop Projects*. Workshop Practice Series Number 39. Special Interest Model Books, Poole.

Chapter 11
Harold Hall, *Dividing*. Workshop Practice Series Number 37. Special Interest Model Books, Poole.

Chapter 15
Harold Hall, *Tool and Cutter Sharpening.*, Workshop Practice Series Number 38. Special Interest Model Books, Poole.

Chapter 16
Shaping machine: set of castings. From:
Stuart Models,
Brave Road, Vale,
Guernsey,
Channel Islands,
UK, GY3 5XA,
tel. 01481 242041/249515,
fax 01481 247912,
email: sales@stuartmodels.com.
Website: www.stuartmodels.com